sustaining lean healthcare programmes

a practical survival guide

MARK EATON ◆ SIMON PHILLIPS

sustaining **lean healthcare** programmes

Book Cover Design & Typesetting by Martin Coote

martincoote@googlemail.com

Cover running figure and lifeline graphic by Boguslaw Mazur/iStockPhoto

Set in *Delicious 10 on 15pt* a typeface by Jos Buivenga

First published in 2008 by;

Ecademy Press

6 Woodland Rise, Penryn,

Cornwall UK TR10 8QD

info@ecademy-press.com

www.ecademy-press.com

Printed and Bound by;

Lightning Source in the UK and USA

Printed on acid-free paper from managed forests. This book is printed on demand, so no copies will be remaindered or pulped.

ISBN 978-1-905823-33-8

A CIP catalogue record for this book is available from the British Library.

Introduction *by Mark Eaton*

Welcome to our book on how to successfully introduce Lean in Healthcare organisations, that I have prepared with my colleague and friend Simon Phillips. This book complements my first book, *Lean for Practitioners* but where the first book focused on the tools and approach to implementing Lean, this book focuses on how to ensure safe and sustainable changes that turn into lasting improvements.

The genesis of this book occurred some years ago when I was heavily involved in delivering Lean programmes for manufacturing on behalf of the UK Government. It became apparent that all was not well in the process of going Lean and I organised some initial research into the causes of Lean 'burnout'.

This research showed that few manufacturing companies were realising the full benefits of their investments in terms of improvement. It also showed that the same percentage of failures were occurring whether the companies were using Lean, Six Sigma or any other form of improvement tools and techniques. In fact this initial research suggested that up to 80% of manufacturing companies were failing to realise the long term benefits from their improvement programme. This was very worrying, especially as the Government was spending millions of pounds of public money on implementing these improvements.

The result of this initial work was rushed into production as a guide for the public sector on Sustaining Lean for Manufacturing. Subsequent work in this area, including additional and more formal pieces of research undertaken by others, demonstrated that we had made some fundamental flaws in our assumptions. At the same time, I met Simon Phillips who was doing pioneering work in the fields of culture change and sustainable performance improvement with a diverse range of organisations including international finance institutions and public organisations, and since 2005 we have been looking at how the lessons we have learnt from manufacturing and elsewhere can be used to avoid 'Lean Burnout' in healthcare organisations. As part of this work we have found a close fit with the issues faced by manufacturing companies as well as some unique issues that only affect healthcare organisations.

From a book born of necessity and expedience in manufacturing, I hope we have created something that will genuinely be of great value to you in your Lean healthcare programme (or because of its general applicability your Six Sigma, Theory of Constraints or 'Whatever Comes Next' healthcare programme).

Please feel free to email us your questions and comments to *sustain@amnis-uk.com*

Contents

1: Where are you on the journey?

Introduction

This chapter focuses on the journey to becoming a Lean Healthcare organisation (which is where Lean is embedded throughout your organisation) but is equally relevant if your vision is to use Lean to fix a few problems in some of your key pathways.

We called this chapter 'Where are you on the journey?' because your progress towards improvement is a journey and not just a single destination. One of the easiest mistakes that people can make is to convert 'Lean' into a series of disconnected projects, each with a finite end. This will generate some results, but will not generate the best result for your organisation.

This chapter introduces you to some of the key points about your journey to Lean that you may have experienced (or can look forward to experiencing if you have not yet started!) as well as introducing you to some of the key people you will meet on your journey.

The journey

The journey to 'Lean' is, as they say in the song, a long and winding road with many twists and turns. If you have already started your journey you may have experienced some of these changes in direction – from the success of your first visual management board and the implementation of new processes that deliver real value, to the first colleague going behind your back to complain about this 'manufacturing fad' called Lean that has no relevance to healthcare organisations.

In this chapter we will explore the journey you may have experienced, either with your Lean Healthcare programme or another one of your improvement activities. It has been written with a touch of humour to emphasise some of the subtleties that you may have missed. However, while it is written with tongue in cheek it still contains some important information that you will need for the task at the end of the chapter, so read it carefully!

Prior to the start

There is a lot of confusion around the organisation about this new initiative called Lean Healthcare. There have been a few scattered reports from other organisations and articles in the Health Service Journal almost every week. People in the corridor may tell you different things. Some say that they are not interested in 'Lean' whatever it may be, others may say that is completely the wrong approach or it is too easy. Someone else might warn you that it is all about turning people into automatons.

The project is launched

You receive an email about a meeting where the Chief Executive is going to announce this new 'Lean' initiative. At the meeting the management team is there in strength and the Service Improvement Lead announces the new programme and what it entails. Sitting on the table is a report from an external consultancy firm that seems to contain lots of complicated graphics and theoretical insights that don't seem to have any relevance to your environment but you are asked whether you would be interested in joining the new 'Lean Team' in a way that leaves you in no doubt that it is expected you will say yes.

The first few fumbling steps

Having been appointed part of the internal Lean Team the first thing you do is read up everything you can about Lean, but all you can find is a lot of hype from other organisations and loads of information about the tools of Lean. Nothing seems to help you to understand **how** you are supposed to do it, or where you are supposed to start! (By the way, if this is true, read our book *Lean for Practitioners*).

After a month or so you have managed to put together a PID (Project Initiation Document) with little or no interest being shown by anyone outside of the Lean team, apart from maybe, the CEO. However, you press on regardless knowing that very few people will read your PID, let alone act on it! Your first reaction, having read something on one of the NHS Institute websites, is to have a crack at running a Rapid Improvement Event as that seems to be the thing to do – but no-one is sure of what this entails and very few people can commit the necessary time to the project.

With little support, your first event goes with a pop (rather than a bang). You manage to achieve a few things, but nothing like what you feel you could have achieved (or the team could have achieved had they been more enthusiastic). Anyway, it is over and you and the rest of the team go back to your office to lick your wounds!

After the first few weeks

Having continued to struggle with getting the Rapid Improvement Events filled; your managers decide to bring in some 'Experts' from a management consultancy firm. Most of their examples seem to come from the manufacturing sector (or from the Civil Service) and they struggle to understand the most basic healthcare terminology and cultural differences.

The consultants do bring some order to the project, but they don't seem very good at passing on their knowledge about how to do Lean and, to be honest, a number of the senior clinicians don't like their attitude.

Month 3

Things have calmed down a bit now and some improvements have been delivered. A number of managers and leaders have moved on to different projects and the pace of change has slowed. Events have been replaced with discussions and meetings that don't seem to achieve much but that take up lots of your time.

Month 6

The CEO suddenly has a burst of enthusiasm and pushes some new people into the Lean project, mostly people who have been displaced and don't have anywhere else to go (or a job to do) so they are not particularly committed. The external consultants are still there and have also started to pass the blame for the events not delivering what your organisation wants on to you and the rest of your team.

Month 9

The CEO is now impatient for results and has piloted a new approach using a different group of management consultant experts and no-one in your team can understand why. Around this time you manage to get yourself onto a useful workshop that explains what you have been doing and all the mistakes become very apparent to you – if only you could go back to the start of the project!

Month 12

The external consultants in Lean left a few weeks ago, but the project had almost come to a halt anyway – partly because no-one had the time for the project or any understanding of what the experts were asking them to do. Some of the people you are working with have left and gone to other organisations and one or two have been posted back into operational roles (where they are much happier). Your role has become one of progress chaser and chief doer as the front-line teams seem to be less and less willing to participate.

The beginning of year 2

You are sitting at your desk scratching your head and not really knowing where to turn – just at that moment you receive an email from a friend telling you to read this new book called *Sustaining Lean Healthcare Programmes* and you do...and so the journey begins!

Is this your experience?

The above is a very tongue in cheek story but it contains a whole range of issues so if you can recognise three or more of the symptoms you will get a lot of value from this book. If you can't recognise three symptoms from the above you might be a best practice site – in which case, when are you free for us to visit?

Process change V Behaviour change

Whatever type of improvement projects you have been involved in, you may have noticed that making changes to processes and pathways is easier than getting them to stick! This is because you are dealing with the difference between Process change and Behaviour change.

- **Process change** – changing the way things are laid out, putting in new protocols and changing the way that services are meant to be delivered.
- **Behaviour change** – this is about getting people to use the new ways of working and to forget that they are 'new'.

Here we are going to use the example of Mark's refuse collection to emphasise the difference between process and behaviour change.

> *"My local council recently insisted that I moved my bins to the road side (a huge 3 metres!) or else they would not empty them.* **(Process Change)**
>
> *"The first week I forgot and they did not take the bins. I forgot the second week too and again they did not take them. Because my wife was annoyed with always having full rubbish bins outside the front door, I eventually remembered to move the bins and after a while it came to be the 'norm' that on Monday mornings I move my bins to the road.* **(Behaviour Change)**"

A key fact is that behaviour change always lags behind process change. If you want people's behaviour to change you need to help them to remember the new ways of working and stop them slipping back into old habits. This takes time! If this is a familiar problem then this book will be of use to you!

Easy in the head – not so easy in the hand!

One of the hardest things to understand about Lean is that it is 'easy in the head' but harder to implement 'in the hand'. Its basic concepts are easy to understand and yet it is much harder to implement and also has a much more strategic focus than it appears at first. This leads to problems with people dismissing your Lean Healthcare programme as minor and tactical, rather than strategic and important. This attitude may undermine your ability to make improvements.

The reality is that Lean is far from easy in the hand if you want to generate safe, sustainable process improvement. Most people only read the first few lines and see that it uses process mapping type tools and this thing called '5S' and assume they have learnt it all. Even after ten years of practising Lean (and having run multi-million pound Lean programmes for the government) we are still learning something new about Lean every day!

If you have encountered this sort of the resistance then this book will be of use to you!

The people you will have met

In your improvement journey (using Lean or any other approach) you will have met a wide range of people, some positive about the process and others less so. Here are some fictional[1] characters possessing various behaviour traits – some positive and some negative – which ones have you met?

> **Dr Mike Walnut** – Mike is passionate about improving patient experience and outcomes and is keen to try anything once. He has heard about Lean, has attended a professional training day on it and is very keen to sing its praises to his colleagues.

> **Dr Sarah Almond** – Sarah is not as keen as Mike on improvement activities and has achieved mixed results in the past. However, she is open to the idea of a new initiative, although she is reserving judgment until she has seen it in action.

> **Dr Gregory Pecan** – Greg is vehemently 'anti' the improvement programme and looks at every email sent

[1]The characters detailed here are not based on any living person and any connection to anyone living or dead is coincidental.

to see what holes he can pick in the programmes. He is always first to challenge the Chief Exec and others about the negative impacts of improvement projects and always comes up with obscure scenarios that would make the new process fail. Greg is quite happy to talk to his professional colleagues about how bad the new process is and is keen to encourage them not to participate.

Anna Pistachio (Matron) – Anna isn't very happy with what is going on but likes to keep her head down and just get on with it. If someone asks her opinion she avoids the question or gives a non-committal response, but never actively takes part in the improvement process and always sees the faults in the solutions designed by others.

Thomas Brazil – Tom works in accounts and is quite motivated by what is going on, but he's really too busy to say so or to take part. When he gets the chance he reads all he can about the improvement process and what the teams have achieved and feels quite motivated about it. In his heart he wishes he had the time to take part. Whenever someone asks him about the process he is always upbeat but also very honest about its limitations.

Rick Hazelnut – Rick who works in the Finance Department is a great connector of people and works well in groups. People describe him as the life and soul of the party and his opinion has real weight in his local group. Rick is a good listener and interprets what he hears well (based on his own experience). If he is positive about something then his passion will often enthuse others, and if he is against something he will make his views known and felt!

Who's Who?

You may or may not recognise the people described above, but they will exist in your organisation. Now it is time for you to guess Who's Who from the list above. Read the descriptions below and then detail which person fits into which character. Our answer is in the Appendices.

Person Type	Description	Who's Who? *your guess*
Advocate	A passionate person who will sing the praises of your improvement programme	
Positive	Someone positive about the programme but who does not shout about it	
Neutral	Someone with an open mind and whose opinions could swing either way	
Negative	Someone who is 'anti' the programme but does not shout about it or try to influence others	
Sniper	Someone who really is 'anti' and is keen to dissuade others from taking part	
Influencer	Someone who could be any of the above categories but who is able also to influence others – sometimes called a natural leader	

The journey to the Land of Lean

The following is an anecdote we frequently use to explain the journey to the Land of Lean – this being a fictional place where the organisation can identify the activities that are preventing them from being effective. It's also where these non-value adding or destructive activities can be tackled using a structured approach and a range of improvement tools. We heard it from someone else, but unfortunately can't remember who it was to be able to attribute it, however it is a very useful description and hope the original author won't mind us adapting the original story and using it.

The Land of Waste

You are setting out in your boat from the Land of Waste on your journey to the Land of Lean. In your boat you have two types of people; Positives (who are rowing the boat) and Neutrals (who are sitting observing). In the water (and trying to grab the oars) are some Negatives.

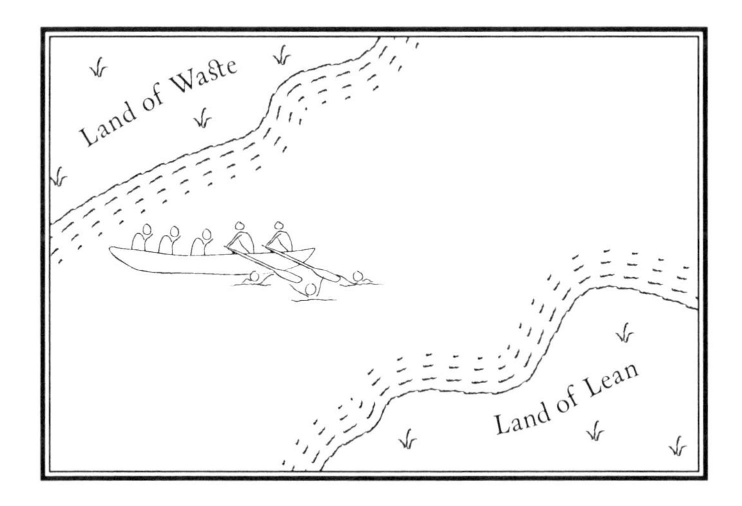

The journey

As you row across the open sea (which at times can be turbulent), some of the Neutrals will jump overboard and become Negatives and some Neutrals will become Positives and start helping you row the boat. In addition, some of the Negatives will get fed up of always being in the cold and will jump into the boat, many becoming Neutrals but a few will become Positives and will be your best rowers.

The Land of Lean

As you approach the Land of Lean you will find you still have Positives and Neutrals in the boat but there are far more Positives helping with the rowing and far fewer Neutrals who are just watching. There will still be the occasional Negative bobbing aimlessly in the water, but they will be the minority. You've reached the Land of Lean. It's not the finish line, but it's a big hurdle to overcome before your journey continues!

So, where are you on the journey?

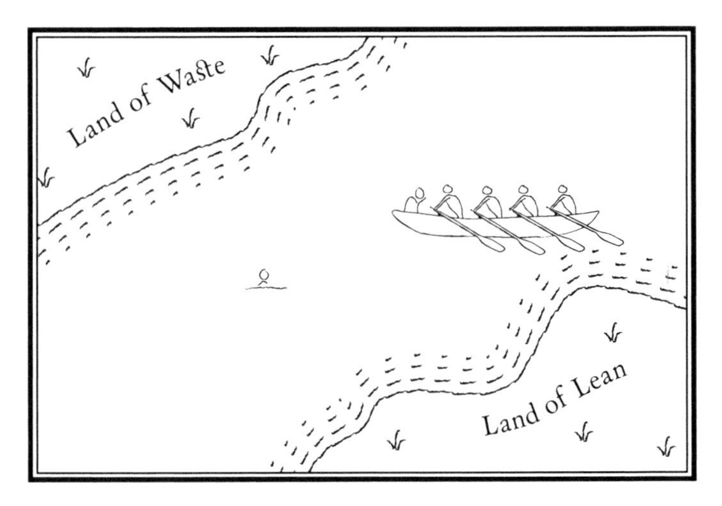

Chapter summary

We've introduced some of the key problems facing Lean healthcare programmes. Do you recognise any of the issues? How good were you at allocating people from the 'Who's Who' into the different categories?

Some of the topics we have covered in this chapter include:

- Process change is different to Behaviour change
- Lean is easy in the Head but not as easy in the Hand
- The types of people you may have met in your journey will include:

  Advocates *Positives* *Neutral*

  Negatives *Snipers* *Influencers*

The journey to Lean is just that – a journey – it is not a destination!

Enjoy the rest of the book!

2: Why do only 25% succeed?

Introduction

In our original research, undertaken in manufacturing, nine success factors were identified that differentiated organisations that were successfully using Lean from those who were being less successful. This was modified by further research undertaken by ourselves in Healthcare, and others in manufacturing and other sectors, and has subsequently been revised down to eight categories.

Our work in the Healthcare sector has confirmed that the same categories are defining success in Lean Healthcare programmes. These eight success categories form the acronym **CRITICAL:**

- Communications
- Resources
- Involvement
- Training
- Implementation
- Compass

- **Achievement**
- **Leadership**

Let's explore these issues in a little more detail and also consider some minor issues that also need to be tackled on the journey.

CRITICAL — The eight elements of success in detail

C – Communications

Successful organisations have a well-constructed communications programme that will perform three functions:

1. Inform the organisation about the programme and what is happening (and why) in an honest and open way
2. Provide opportunities for two-way dialogue with staff
3. Celebrate success at every opportunity

Focus first on achieving these three objectives. In addition, take great care to ensure the message is consistent across all the various media and remember that the communications programme may also be useful in performing other functions such as informing patients and other stakeholders about the programme and providing comments on targets/measures of success.

A communications programme does not just consist of a magazine or a weekly email. The best communications programmes normally consist of a variety of activities including:

- Internal newsletters
- Forums/meetings/awareness sessions
- Meetings with the board
- Staff briefings & Open letters
- Press releases, Notice boards & Emails

Our main suggestion is to keep it simple. The more complex you make the communications programme, the more difficult it will be to achieve a consistent message. You need to get the balance right between providing different access routes for the information, with the need for consistency across all routes. This area needs careful attention.

R – Resources

The allocation of appropriate resources, in terms of time and people rather than cash, is frequently thought to be the most important reason for success, and the most common reason for failure when solving a problem.

Time and again we hear of projects that have stalled because the only person working on it is in an office at the far end of the organisation that already has three or four jobs to do and is not openly supported by their manager.

For your Lean Healthcare programme to be truly successful you need to consider what resources you are willing to provide. Some examples being used by successful organisations include:

- A dedicated service improvement team
- The support of a wide group of people from across the organisation

- Sufficient time allocated for people to meet and resolve problems
- Senior clinical engagement

We have found that interminable weekly meetings rarely deliver the right results for the organisation and often no long-term improvements result. However, it is easier to organise weekly meetings than to allocate half a day to solve a problem properly! Is this your experience?

I – Involvement

The third of the eight items that differentiates successful organisations is the involvement of all the right people. This means thinking outside the function, outside the department and often outside the organisation, to make sure that all the people who significantly influence the issue are involved.

A common mistake is restricting an improvement project to one department or 'bounding' it to avoid involving people from other organisations, or even another department. Examples of this include 'bounding' a project at the doors of A&E so that you do not need to involve the Ambulance Trusts or anyone from Primary Care, or only focusing on 'Med Secs' and ignoring the impact of ward staff, health records or others.

This failure to involve the people who influence the problem (or at the very least have something valuable to add) means that the team is immediately disempowered to deal with the problems. The project can often degenerate into a series of statements about how other organisations or departments (who are not involved) need to improve – but how can they, when no-one communicates with them?

The most successful organisations are thinking 'end to end' about their problems, looking to involve all the key people, departments and organisations who are involved in the pathway or process, or who influence the success of that area. That is how they achieve safe sustainable process improvement.

T – Training

The most successful organisations are doing appropriate levels of training and are ensuring that the teaching is quickly followed up with some practical experience. Misquoting a common phrase:

> *Tell* me and I will listen, *show* me and I will believe, but allow me to *do it* and I will understand

Too much training is typified by sending people on lengthy courses with no follow through in the work place or little implementation related or practical exercises built into the training. Extensive in-house training courses that are not linked to any practical implementation experience create the same problems.

Very often, too little training occurs in the rush to make improvements and includes failing to give the participants the basic skills required to lead a Lean Programme. In our experience, the basic skills/concepts that people need to understand are:

- Value & the 7 wastes (+1)
- 5 principles of Lean (including explaining Flow and Pull)
- 5S+1 (visual control/management)
- Set-up reduction (SMED: Single Minute Exchange of Die)
- Basic Change Management
- Mistake proofing (aka Poka Yoke)

In addition, depending on where you are in the journey, you might want people to know about skills, such as Value Stream Mapping, that may be relevant to the specific problem that requires a solution at that time. The short list above should be treated as a minimum skill set.

I – Implementation

Where do we start with this? Organisations go about implementing improvements in different ways and there is little in common in the programmes of improvement between even the most successful organisations.

However, here are the top ten issues that we believe define successful implementation:

1. A clear vision for what you are attempting to achieve
2. A focus on redesigning the pathway from end to end
3. The appropriate use of Rapid Improvement Events, Focused Improvement Teams (aka Continuous Improvement Teams) and similar programmes of improvement
4. An effective pace of change – not too fast and not too slow
5. Strong management engagement in the process

6. A process of continuously reviewing and improving processes to ensure you do not slip back
7. A focus on short term gains **and** long-term change
8. Dealing with resistance 'head-on' and not allowing 'Snipers' to derail the process unnecessarily
9. Celebrating successes and ensuring that lessons are learnt and shared
10. An acceptance that the journey to improvement is not a straight line and occasionally problems will occur (one step forwards and two steps back)

So what are the unsuccessful organisations doing wrong? An absence of any of the items listed above in the improvement project is a recipe for disaster, as is a singular focus on using one tool (such as Rapid Improvement Events (RIEs)) when more appropriate approaches would suit the organisation and the situation better.

C – Compass

Knowing where you are heading is essential. It entails setting out the vision for your improvement programme, what you want to achieve (and why), what it will mean for the organisation and an outline of the plan for the improvement process (at least for the first six months). You will notice the real value of the compass when your programme goes off course as you can constantly refer back to True North on your compass and realign your activity accordingly.

A – Achievement

The sense of achievement is a powerful motivator. It is felt when moving from discussion into action and achieving results in the quickest possible time after the start of the programme.

That's it – no magic formula – just simply doing something and keeping moving forward!

L – Leadership

Leadership (at all levels) plays an enormous part in ensuring that improvement programmes are a success and that improvements are sustained. The best organisations have the following attributes in common:

1. Leaders (at all levels) directly involved in the programme at every stage
2. The *leader* (the top person in the organisation) taking part in celebrating success and setting direction
3. A board level Improvement Sponsor to make sure that roadblocks are overcome/fixed
4. A process of reviewing progress and ensuring that things do not slip back
5. An organised and cross-functional Improvement group or board', with clinical representation as well as representation from across the organisational grades
6. Leaders holding themselves accountable for releasing resources and setting the pace of change
7. Effective delegation of responsibility so that the teams are empowered to make the necessary changes.

Other opportunity areas

In addition to the eight **CRITICAL** areas outlined above, there are also a few areas that need to be considered and these include:

1. **Bringing new people in** – sometimes termed on-boarding of new people into an area and ensuring they work to the process standards adopted by the group as a whole, rather than importing bad practice.

2. **IT systems** – inappropriate or poorly designed IT systems can derail programmes. They need to be manipulated to ensure they add value rather than detract from the success. It is important to consider the way that IT will impact your planned changes and, even better, how you can integrate your planned improvements with existing IT frameworks. Getting IT on-board and excited about the changes (after all, change generally keeps IT departments in business) is a very useful tactic.

3. **HR policies** – HR policies will need to be changed when an improvement occurs to ensure the change is safe and sustainable. Just like IT, involving HR in the programme will shorten the implementation timescales as the HR team will often anticipate how the improvement can be embedded into the existing organisational policies and procedures. Retro fitting your requirements is always inefficient in both time and cost.

4. **Snipers** – some people will hold a deep resentment about the process of improvement – from a Clinical Consultant worried about losing their Med Sec/PA, to a Director concerned about their area's problems being exposed to the world. Some of these people will talk about it to you

directly, but some of them will work against the programme and will need to be tackled head-on before they spread too much doom and gloom. We cover this later in this book.

Removing the 'old shoes'

One more area to consider in this chapter is removing the ability for people to go back – which could mean anything; from removing a wall to taking away all green pens to something really dramatic such as redeploying staff.

The most successful organisations remove the opportunity of mistakes occurring by ensuring old (and bad) habits cannot creep back in!

The key is to ensure the process remains safe. This removal process is often gradual and there is always a need for a contingency plan to be put in place (particularly in high risk processes). However, it does mean preventing people from making mistakes by removing their ability to 'go back'. We will discuss this using an anecdote of 'new shoes'!

When you implement a change you are effectively giving people new shoes and these may not feel as good as their favourite, comfortable and worn-in shoes. It does not matter that the old shoes are slightly scuffed, have been repaired and let water in – the fact is that they feel better than the new shoes and when people are in a rush they will always revert to their old shoes. Many of us have done it; you buy a new pair of trainers but insist on wearing the old ones into the ground before being forced to throw them away. We tell ourselves that the old ones are more comfortable, easier to get on and sometimes even better than the new ones!

Throwing away the old shoes makes it impossible to step back into them!

Chapter summary

The most successful organisations consider the following eight elements in their improvement programmes. As we have said before, they form the acronym **CRITICAL:**

- **Communications** – having a robust and two way communication process
- **Resources** – allocating the right amount of time and human resource (and cash)
- **Involvement** – involving all the key people in the pathway/ process
- **Training** – neither too much nor too little and always focused on practical application over simple theory
- **Implementation** – having a robust plan, map and implementation programme
- **Compass** – setting out your vision for the process
- **Achievement** – moving from discussion into action
- **Leadership** – having leaders who engage effectively in the process

There are other minor areas that need to be considered to be truly successful, but the most important thing is to consider is taking away the 'Old Shoes' so that you reduce the ability of people to slip back into old habits!

3: Going Lean

Introduction

Having explored what most successful organisations are doing to ensure their Lean Healthcare programme delivers the desired results, this chapter outlines how to turn this list of things to be done into a structured plan of action.

When implementing Lean in Healthcare we use the PRISM Model[2] as shown below:

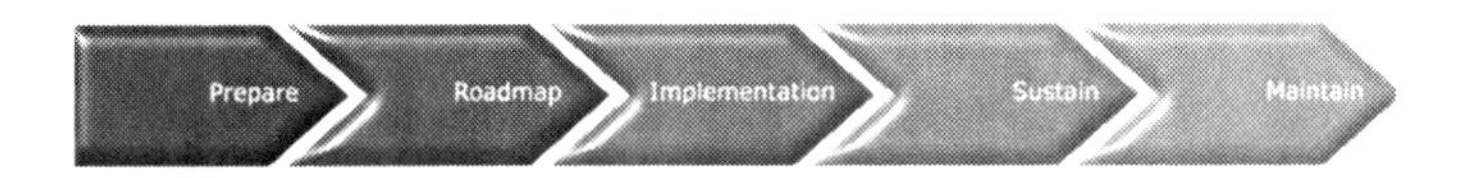

The five steps in the PRISM model are outlined as:

- **Prepare** – get the organisation ready for the improvement
- **Roadmap** – set out the plan for improvement
- **Implementation** – make the improvements happen
- **Sustain** – embed the changes in the organisation
- **Maintain** – prepare the organisation for the next improvement bound

[2]The PRISM Model is a registered trademark of Amnis Ltd and is freely available for use on the basis that its source is acknowledged.

The steps involved in PRISM are explained in more detail below.

PRISM Step 1: Prepare *(the organisation)*

Prior to any actual implementation activity it is essential that organisations prepare themselves effectively. We recognise that there are five activities that should occur as part of a Prepare phase, namely:

1. Scope the improvement programme
2. Begin development of your internal change agents
3. Communicate with your staff (and allow them to contribute to the programme)
4. Gather relevant data about the organisation, pathway or process
5. Establish an improvement group

We have outlined below how the scoping of an improvement process could be undertaken along with an outline for a Change Agent Development (CAD) Programme. In addition, we have provided a short outline for the key components of a successful improvement group.

Scoping session

A scoping session is perhaps the most important Lean event you will undertake. The scoping session encapsulates the compelling need for the organisation to change that will be communicated to the staff. The outline agenda for a scoping session is outlined below and a guide is provided in the appendices:

- Agree the boundaries of the programme of work
- Identify the compelling need for the organisation or pathway to be improved
- Identify the 3-7 measures of success that will be used
- Identify who needs to be involved in the programme
- Identify what must not be touched during the change process, the boundaries and key risks
- Identify what data needs to be gathered
- Identify the key roles in the improvement process
- Set timescales and allocate supporting resources
- Identify how the programme will be communicated

CAD *(Change Agent Development)* programme

All Healthcare organisations should consider the development of the skills and abilities of their change agents (these change agents could simply be your Service Improvement Team or a mix of this team and others who undertake Service Improvement work on a part time basis) as a high priority. Typical CAD Programmes will combine both practical experience of and training in Lean principles. Additional training and development activities will be focused on helping change agents to understand how to motivate, guide and coach others, as well as manage and measure the improvement process.

The topics that could be covered by a CAD Programme include:

- Lean skills (including how to run events)
- Presentation & negotiation skills

- Managing Change & Facilitation skills
- Coaching & Mentoring others
- Managing Risk & Patient Safety
- Train the Trainer skills

Within your improvement programme, you might want to think about the development needs of the different improvement groups who will exist within your organisation, which will include:

- **The Aware** – people who have had an introduction to Lean and the core principles (plus details of how they can implement improvements in their own area), but who are unlikely to be involved in Lean events in the next few months.
- **Users** – people who have participated in one or a few Lean events or might reasonably be expected to be involved in an event during the next 4-8 months.
- **Practitioners (or Change Practitioners)** – key staff who have gained experience in a wide range of events, but who have an operational role (i.e. they are not full time change agents) and who are expected to take on a leadership role (at any level) in an improvement process.
- **Change Agents** – Highly experienced key staff that act as a central resource and advisory team to local improvement events run by Change Practitioners. They will facilitate improvements, carry out training and awareness sessions for all other staff and will be the repository of best practice in the organisation.

Improvement group

Assembling an improvement group during the Prepare phase is essential. This group will take a management role in setting the direction of the programme, overcoming barriers and monitoring performance. Some of the key elements that will make for a successful improvement group include:

- Having senior representation (including an Improvement Sponsor at Board Level)
- Having a broad representation across the organisation
- Involving clinical staff at various levels
- Having a defined agenda covering:
    - Current progress
    - Barriers to improvement
    - Lessons learned & sharing knowledge
- Meeting regularly and actually achieving something
- Having guest attendees from different departments, organisations and other sectors

PRISM Step 2: Roadmap *(the process)*

Having prepared your organisation for Lean, you will need to roadmap how your critical pathways and processes operate. This step needs to focus on the following activities:

1. Redesigning the Pathway (often using Value Stream Mapping techniques)
2. Preparing for implementation

You should also remember to:

1. Continue the development of your change agents
2. Continue communicating with your staff

In this section we will specifically look at the process of redesigning pathways using Value Stream Mapping using something we have termed a Value Stream Analysis Event (VSE).

Value Stream Analysis Event (VSE)

A Value Stream Analysis Event (VSE) creates a future state for a pathway or process. A VSE normally occurs in three phases spread over nine weeks with the actual event week lasting from two to five days (depending on the complexity of the issue). We have outlined the VSE process below and provided an example guide to a VSE in the Appendices:

1. **Weeks 1-4 (Pre-VSE Phase)** – gathering the data required to undertake the VSE and preparing the team
2. **Week 5 (event week)** – undertaking the actual VSE which breaks down as follows:
    A. Opening brief – given by a senior manager
    B. Understand current state
    C. Create a 'Blue Sky' vision
    D. Plan a realistic future state
    E. Closing brief – given by the team to their managers
3. **Week 6-9 (post-VSE phase)** – preparing for the implementation of the new future state

A VSE will involve the use of a range of Lean tools including:

- Process analysis: mapping, hand-off charts & string diagrams
- Data analysis & charting
- 'Blue Sky' designs
- Future state maps

PRISM Step 3: Implementation *(and review)*

Following on from the Roadmap Phase, you should consider how you will implement the improvements. Whilst there is a bit of a fixation on 'Rapid Improvement Events' in Healthcare, it is not the be-all-and-end-all of improvement activities. This phase could consist of the following activities

1. Rapid Improvement Events (RIE)
2. Rapid Planning Events (RPE)
3. Focused Improvement Teams (FIT) (sometimes also called Continuous Improvement Teams)
4. Project Teams

In addition, you should also be considering:

5. Continuation of the training for your change agents
6. Celebration of successes
7. Progress gates – reviews of what has been achieved and how that affects your future improvement plans

In this section we will specifically look at Rapid Improvement Events and Rapid Planning Events as well as Focused Improvement Teams and a summary of a Progress Gate:

Rapid Improvement Events (RIE)

A Rapid Improvement Event (RIE) is used to improve a process in a practical and structured way and will usually focus on a specific area within a Pathway (or Value Stream). An RIE consists of three phases spread over nine weeks, with the actual event week lasting between one and five days depending on the complexity of the issues/areas to be tackled. The process for an RIE is outlined below:

1. **Week 1-4 (Prepare phase)** – gathering data, preparing the area and team for the improvement event
2. **Week 5 (event week)** – the physical implementation of improvements, which normally occurs as:
    A. Opening brief
    B. Understanding current state
    C. Design new solution
    D. Implement & test new solution
    E. Closing brief
3. **Week 6-9 (bedding in phase)** – testing, improving and embedding the improvements

The tools of an RIE will vary widely but could include:

- Process maps, Hand-Off Charts and String Diagrams
- Paper layouts
- Process at a glance
- DMT (Design, Move, Test)
- 5S/Visual management
- Kanban (Pull systems)

- Standard work
- Set-Up Reduction aka SMED (Single Minute Exchange of Die)/ Total Productive Maintenance (TPM)\

If you are interested, we would be happy to share a Client Guide to running RIEs, just drop us an email to *sustain@amnis-uk.com* with 'RIE Guide' as the email title.

Rapid Planning Events (RPE)

The mantra for process transformation in the healthcare sector should be that it is safe for all. Some processes are too high risk to move straight to an RIE (where things physically change) and an RPE (Rapid Planning Event) is an intermediate activity between a Value Stream Mapping Event (VSE) that we encountered earlier and a Rapid Improvement Event and is designed to de-risk a process. The RPE consists of three phases spread over nine weeks with the actual event week lasting from one to five days depending on the complexity of the problem to be solved.

The RPE process is outlined below:

1. **Weeks 1-4 (Prepare phase)** – gathering data, preparing the area and team for the planning event
2. **Week 5 (event week)** – the actual RPE itself, which breaks down into the following steps:
    - A. Opening brief
    - B. Gather data & understand current process
    - C. Design & test new process
    - D. Plan implementation
    - E. Closing brief

3. **Weeks 6–9 (Planning & implementation phase)** – preparing for the resulting improvement event (RIE)

Because RPEs vary widely, the tools used will vary too, but often include:

- Process maps, Hand-off charts and string diagrams
- Paper layouts & process at a glance
- 'Plan-its'
- Process backbone & ribs
- Design 5 & FMEA (Failure Modes & Effects Analysis)

If you are interested, we would be happy to share a Client Guide to running RPEs, just drop us an email to *sustain@amnis-uk.com* with 'RPE Guide' as the email title.

Focused Improvement Teams (FIT)

A Focused Improvement Team (or Continuous Improvement Team) is a team focused on continuously improving a process that has been through some form of a Lean Event or is a team established to tackle a specific issue, which is not suited to an RIE or RPE approach. As such, it is difficult to state a structure or the tools that will be used by FIT teams, but these teams are essential if you want to embed changes into your organisation.

Progress gate

It is important to review the progress being made by the teams on a regular basis. We normally suggest doing this at least quarterly and to use the 'Improvement Group' as the basis for the review process. A Progress Gate is different to a general progress meeting (which we would suggest occurs monthly). The Progress Gate is fundamentally a 'stake in the ground' to ensure that the programme is still on track, that the overall plan is still valid and to collate the results achieved so far.

A typical Progress Gate agenda will be:

- Review of activities to date
- Review of lessons learnt, achievements and obstacles
- Review of the future state and any emerging information that alters it
- Review of the forward plan of activity (including the communications plan)
- Next steps & changes to the plan

PRISM Step 4: Sustain *(the improvement)*

In this section we start to explore the key differences that enable the most successful organisations to realise the full benefits of their improvement programme (and also start exploring new territory not covered in our original book *Lean for Practitioners*).

We will explore the top five issues that will help you embed the improvements you have implemented during your Lean Healthcare programme.

Daily improvements

Successful, safe and sustainable Lean in Healthcare programmes depends on focusing on continuous improvement activities. The best way of achieving this is for teams to meet quickly at the start of every day or shift and focus on the problems of the previous day and how they will make the process better today. The danger is for these sessions to become moans and groans and they will need some steering at first from your internal change agents.

However, it is important that the change agents are not press ganged to do the work of improving the process of the team. Despite the stress it will cause to start with, the front-line team needs to own the improvements.

Management Audits

In addition to a focus on daily improvements, managers play a big role in embedding the improvements and this is best achieved by active participation in management audits of the process. This can be based around our $5S^{+1}$ audit shown in the Appendices, coupled with an opportunity for staff to feedback what they have achieved to their managers. Again, it is important that these sessions do not become an opportunity to off-load the problems onto the managers. Managers can best achieve this by adopting an approach designed to help the team to find the answers for themselves.

Communication & Coaching

Frequent communication about the progress of your Lean Healthcare programme and the achieved results is an excellent way of involving people and also increases the rate of change. It provides your team with an opportunity to participate in the process by contributing ideas for improvement in their areas.

Coupled with these on-going communication activities will be the need for 1-2-1 coaching for some of the key people involved – including those who are nervous about the process, as well as those who are expected to lead the improvements. Coaching, and sometimes mentoring, can dramatically improve the performance of your key change agents and ensure that the learning they have acquired is embedded.

Removal of the 'old shoes'

Having made the changes, removing the ability of others to go back to the way they used to work (removing the 'old shoes') will help to embed the changes and ensure that people are not in a position to make mistakes by reverting to old (and bad) habits!

Dealing with Snipers & Roadblocks

Sadly, as soon as you start to achieve results you will also bring out the negative elements in your organisation. A very small percentage (<1%) of your organisation will make a significant amount of noise and will place unnecessary boulders in the road (roadblocks). You will find yourself being more and more drawn into discussions with people who only seem to be interested in pursuing their own agenda to the detriment of the improvement programme.

Some of these concerns will be valid and some of those who appear to be Snipers are actually just interested in how the programme works. After a while you will be able to spot the difference between those who are enthusiastic, but difficult and those who are, well... just difficult!

What you do with them is up to you, but our suggestion is that they need to be moved out the way or isolated – for the sake of the many people who are interested in getting on and making your improvement programmes a success!

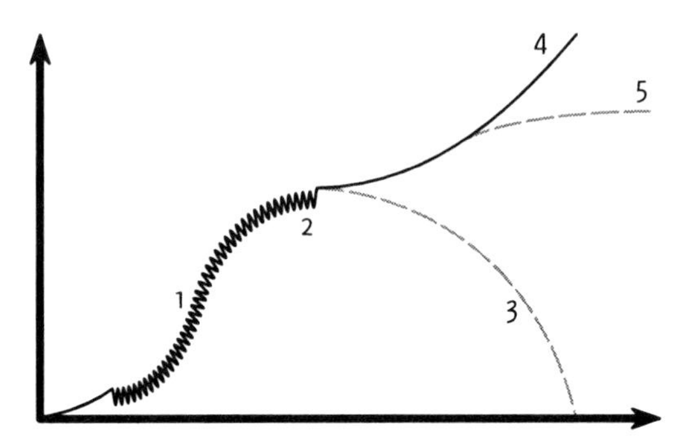

PRISM Step 5: Maintain *(the momentum)*

The last of the five steps of the PRISM model is maintaining the momentum of improvement. The first pass of your Lean Healthcare programme will generate significant results (assuming the improvements are sustained) and will overcome a significant amount of inertia - but how do you keep it going?

The answer is simple – go back to the beginning and start again! Hold a new scoping meeting, a new future state and more Rapid Improvement Events – keep the pressure up and the communication flowing!

The figure above shows what the real journey to Lean in Healthcare feels like. The five numbers on the journey are outlined below:

1. After an initial start up period, the organisation will get into the process of improvement. This feels very bumpy as

assumptions are challenged and people start to resist and support in equal measure. It is important to not allow minor set-backs to slow or stop the progress. This is when the processes are being changed and people are getting used to new ways of working and you should expect lots of 'noise'.

2. After a while (sometimes after quite a few months), the noise will reduce and it will feel like the process is slowing down – but in reality it is just becoming 'the way things are done' as improved processes finally become changed behaviours and this is when you will start to realise the improvements.
3. At this point your managers will move onto the next 'great thing' and this can lead to people reverting back to their previous behaviour. To avoid this happening it is important to maintain your commitment during this phase.
4. Having reached a new level of working, the organisation may decide to push on and build on the momentum, knowledge and improvement culture they have established. This is about maintaining the momentum of change and re-scoping, doing a new design and moving forward on new events but…
5. It is perfectly understandable that some teams want to maintain the new performance standard and not go any further. This should be challenged, as Lean transformation is actually a process of continuous improvement. Quite often, standing still can be more difficult, and take more effort, than continuing to improve and there is always a risk of slipping backwards as new external forces undermine the gains you have made.

Fitting it all together

Activities undertaken within the PRISM Model are designed to fit together in multiple ways. Here we will explore two of these different ways of fitting it all together.

Within a single pathway

The diagram below shows an organisation making improvements in a single pathway. Having made one pass through the PRISM process, it is possible to start again and make just as much improvement the second time! This may seem counter-intuitive but the reality is that having done the process once the team understand what to look for and are braver at tackling the more difficult issues.

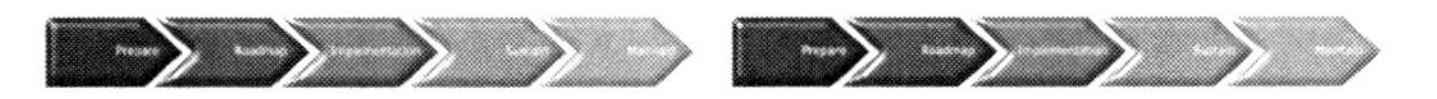

Within multiple pathways

Applying PRISM is not limited to the application in a single pathway. It is possible to apply them to a variety of programmes concurrently, although for every new pathway being tackled the workload of monitoring the progress for the improvement group increases.

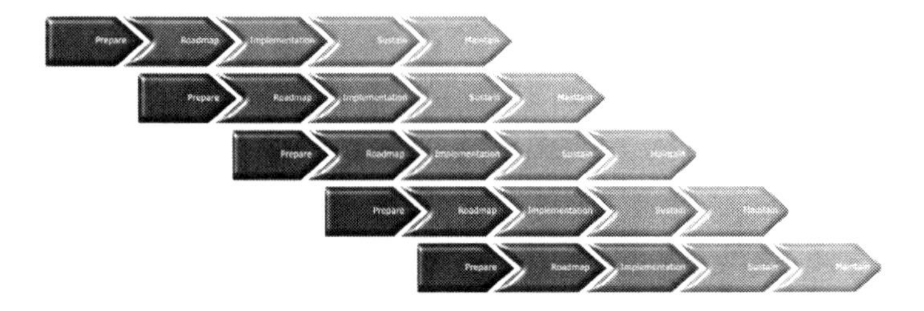

The diagram above shows multiple pathways being started at regular points after the first one. However, whilst this is possible, we suggest that you start with one pathway as after you have implemented some of the changes (and ironed out the problems) you can start to go faster and faster as shown in the diagram below:

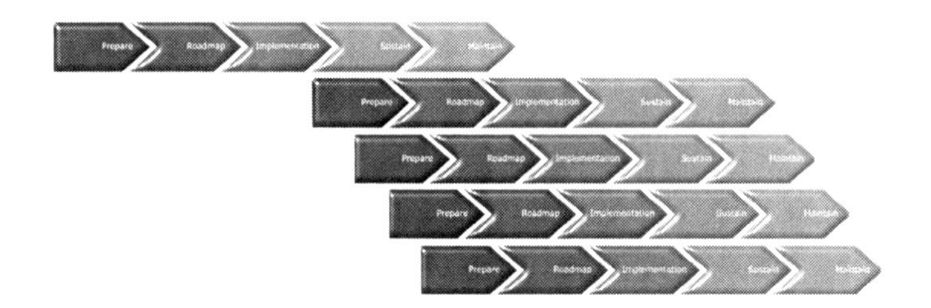

Chapter summary

This chapter has focused on the process for implementing Lean and has built on our other Lean Healthcare focused book 'Lean for Practitioners'. To be successful, Lean needs to be applied using a structured improvement approach such as PRISM™ which stands for:

- **Prepare** (the organisation)
- **Roadmap** (the process)
- **Implementation** (and review)
- **Sustain** (the improvement)
- **Maintain** (the momentum)

Some of the techniques that underpin the PRISM model include:

- Scoping sessions
- Change agent development programmes
- Improvement groups

- Value Stream Analysis Events (VSE)
- Rapid Improvement Events (RIE)
- Rapid Planning Events (RPE)
- Focused Improvement Teams (FIT)
- Progress gates

PRISM programmes do not exist in a vacuum and it is possible to run multiple programmes either within one area or across the organisation.

4: The top ten signs of a failing programme

Introduction

In this chapter we explore the top ten warning signs that indicate that your Lean Healthcare programme might be going 'off track' and that it needs some swift action or even a bit of TLC to bring it back on course!

For each of the following ten warning signs we have tried to summarise what you will experience for each of them as well as trying to rationalise why these events occur and what you might be able to do to correct the issue. This is not presented as a definitive list, but is based on our experience of talking to many hundreds of individuals who have had problems with improvement programmes. We would welcome your experiences in this area to continue the process of learning how to do this even better!

Warning sign 1: *Loss of leadership interest*

What you will experience

Leaders suddenly fail to turn up to event briefings, meetings, celebrations and other activities related to your improvement programme. You will also notice a reduction in the enthusiasm and frequency of communications about the programme and a change of emphasis, possibly accompanied by a new initiative being launched which does not seem to sit with (or build on) the previous work on your Lean Healthcare programme (more of this later!). Your requests for management input will become less effective and you will find that the teams involved in the improvement process become more resistant to the activities. Can you blame them? They sense the change of management focus; and if their managers are not interested, why should they be?

Why it happens

There are a number of reasons why leaders (at all levels) could lose interest in the programme, ranging from a new government policy to the simple fact that they are planning to leave the organisation. Here are some of the main reasons why Leaders sometimes lose interest in improvement programmes:

1. **External factors:** An outside influence such as a new government policy, unexpected change in the external environment (such as a new reporting structure or change to reporting processes).

2. **Internal factors:** An internal influence such as a new senior manager or change in organisational dynamic – such as significant internal resistance from clinicians.

3. **Personal issues:** Such as a change in home situation or work situation (most commonly, they are leaving – not always voluntarily).

4. **Change in beliefs:** Change in the beliefs of the leaders concerned, either believing that Lean has had its day or that

the job is done. In addition, it could be that the feedback has not been as good (or bad) as expected and this results in a change in behaviour.

These are the most common reasons that we have encountered. However, there are many other potential drivers for the change of behaviour of Leaders at any level; the key is not to make assumptions.

What you can do about it

Be clear from the outset what commitment is required from leaders (remembering it is one of the CRITICAL issues mentioned earlier) and how they need to behave (and for how long). This will often avoid some of the problems in these areas (although you will never be able to change their desire to leave the organisation if they want to!) If these requirements have not been set out (or even if they have) and it is going wrong, then you MUST meet with the managers/leaders concerned (starting with the most senior person involved in the programme). The purpose of this meeting is to discuss their views about the programme and how their behaviour affects you and the programme. If you have any other objective feedback from the team about how they feel about the sudden absence of managerial/leadership input then provide that too! If this session does not result in a change in leadership support, seek another, more positive, leader immediately and then move to isolate or supplant the previous leader. This is important, as an inactive leader can cause significant damage to your improvement programme, even if they are not proactively working against you.

Warning sign 2: *Loss of team input*

What you will experience

Your Lean Healthcare programme will be ticking along nicely and getting results (to varying degrees) and suddenly you will notice that team members stop participating, either by going silent (which may include not responding to emails) or simply not turning up or joining in. In addition, you will notice a change in the way that people speak to you about how they feel about the programme as well as a variety of excuses being used to delay activities.

Why it happens

Again, like leadership disengagement there could be a variety of issues driving this sort of behaviour and the most common ones that we have encountered include:

1. **The rumour mill:** Rumours that the changes will lead to job cuts or a change in the role (or loss of the role) of the team members.
2. **Peer pressure:** From either within or outside the team. This could be driven by a lack of understanding or other people's bad experiences.
3. **Pace of change:** The feeling that they are not making as much progress as they could (or conversely that it is all going too fast).
4. **Personal beliefs:** The feeling that their views are not being listened to or that changes are being imposed on them (they are being 'Leaned'). Alternatively, there could be a lack of confidence in the solutions that have been designed, including a feeling that they will introduce additional patient safety risks.

What you can do about it

In the first instance it is important to re-engage your advocates (positives) in the process and get their support to help you get the team back on track. Explaining to people at the start of the process that it is not a 'straight line' to success and that sometimes they will make two steps forward and one step back will help when people start to experience concerns (or at least allow you to be seen as a prophet by foretelling what will happen). Also, explaining that not all Lean Healthcare Programmes have been successful and why yours will be different, with its focus on sustainable improvement, will provide them with logical counter arguments to the rumours they may hear.

However, the biggest and most obvious thing that can be done when the team starts to drift away (either physically or mentally) is to:

1. Coach them back on track by helping them see what has been (or could be) achieved
2. Listen to their concerns (and do something to address them)
3. Ensure their managers remain enthusiastic about the processes.

Warning sign 3: *Rolling roadblock*

What you will experience

You will be in the implementation phase of a programme and will have redesigned the pathways and will suddenly experience a reversal as people start bringing out obstacles that did not occur during the Pathway Redesign exercise in the Roadmap phase. People will start finding more and more reasons not to take action and every time you knock down a roadblock, you will find that another has been erected in front of you. You will find people making comments such as, *"Come on then, tell us how we can do our job more effectively."*

Why it happens

Some of the reasons have already been explored in warning sign 2 above, but specifically you can expect a rolling roadblock situation to be driven by:

- **Failed engagement:** Failing to engage key clinical (or other) staff during the redesign phase. These people have something valid to say about the new process, but feel that their views are not wanted. They then resist the proposed changes – sometimes for real reasons and sometimes **because of a lack of understanding.**
- **Sniper Attack:** The silent enemies of any process improvement will often wait until the changes are about to happen (or have already started) to start finding reasons for the process to fail. Some will do this because they have genuine concerns about the process whilst others will do it just to 'spite' the organisation, or because they feel sidelined.
- **Under involvement:** If you decided to redesign a pathway during the redesign phase without having the involvement of all departments/organisations affected (or if the person sent from a department or organisation is not strong enough) you will find that people resist because of a lack of understanding or because of 'Not Invented Here' Syndrome.

What you can do about it

If the Rolling Roadblock is being driven by any of the issues outlined in the 'Warning Sign 2' section above you need to follow those rules. If it is caused by anything described in this section, you will need to do some 'patching up' and communication to get people back on side. It is vital to maintain the support of your leadership team, as it will be able to help overcome some of the barriers within (and without) the organisation. Especially as they will hear lots of negative feedback from both Snipers and disengaged clinicians and they will need to know what is going on to be able to support your Lean Healthcare Programme effectively.

Warning sign 4: *Silly season (Is that banana active or inactive?)*

What you will experience

The phrase 'Is that banana active or inactive?' is taken from a headline report about the use of Lean in the Public Sector. It is an example of silly season comments from either participants in a Lean event or practitioners of Lean who do not really understand what it is all about. You will experience people being very silly about Lean by labeling racks with the word 'rack' and painting lines on the floor and writing the word 'line'. You will find people making throwaway comments about how they will 'tidy up because it is their Lean day/event' which means that things are just being moved out of the way until you have turned your back. You will also see this silliness in some Lean Healthcare programmes being run by people obsessed by the theory of Lean who start putting the theories ahead of the practical applications.

Why the silly season happens

If you are working with Lean Healthcare practitioners who approach Lean as a box of tools, or who have not got a significant amount of experience, they will approach Lean in a very rigid manner. If the resistance is coming from the team themselves it is often driven by a lack of understanding on their part of what Lean is really about.

What you can do about it

One way of avoiding this is to only work with people (including external management consultants) who have a breadth of experience of implementing improvements. Alternatively you can provide suitable case studies to the teams involved to show them what Lean is really about (as well as communicating with them on a regular basis about what is going on elsewhere in the organisation). Sometimes though you will just have to grin and bear it!

Warning sign 5: *No sustainability*

What you will experience

You turn your back and everything that has been achieved has been dismantled and returned to the old state (the way things were before you started). Alternatively, you will have helped the team establish disciplines to keep the ball rolling (such as daily 5S[+1] audits) but find that the only time they ever do them is when you are there to prompt them, or even worse, when they give you the form to fill in for yourself!

Why it happens

The main reasons this happens are:

1. **Lack of understanding:** Not everyone in the team fully understands why the new processes are there or they believe that these new Lean processes are not worth the effort.
2. **Wrong systems used:** The systems you put in place need to be simple, quick and easy to recall – making them visual helps, but does not compensate for lengthy systems (such as daily continuous improvement groups or similar lengthy activities)
3. **Insufficient time:** Whatever happens, the first few weeks after a Lean event will require continual input from you (and your managers) to make sure that things do not slip and that visual charts are updated and any audits put in place are followed.
4. **Removing the 'old shoes':** If the team still has the ability to do it the old way, they will often revert to it through habit. Your job will be to safely remove the 'old shoes' from the team.

What you can do about it

Some of the solutions have already been referred to in the previous section. Your role will be to ensure that everyone in the area understands why the processes have changed and the benefits it will bring to the organisation. In addition, you will also be the key to ensuring that the right systems are used to ensure the changes are embedded This could include; daily $5S^{+1}$ audits (see the Appendices), 5 minute pre/post shift meetings, management meetings, control charts or visual control boards. You will also need the support of the manager and any influencers in the group to help you remove the 'old shoes' safely.

Warning sign 6:

Where has all the knowledge gone?

What you will experience

All the people who have been through significant Lean Healthcare events are no longer in the area (or the organisation) and those that are left only have a passing knowledge of the Lean process.

Why it happens

Good people with lots of experience of improving pathways are a valuable commodity in the Healthcare sector. If the number of people trained to do Lean is not significant then you are at risk when two or three key people leave. It could also be that Lean has become 'uncool' in your organisation and all the experienced people have distanced themselves from it and no longer wish to engage in the process – this last problem relates to the issues surrounding Leaders disengaging (Warning sign 1).

What you can do about it

Ensure that at least 0.3% (with a minimum of 3) and ideally more of the people in the pathway gain sufficient knowledge to be classed as change agents of Lean with around 8% trained to be practitioners within the first year (Note: we will explore the definitions for both of these groups in more detail later). This will give you a strong base for success and also reduce the impact of one or two people leaving. You should also consider running an on-going programme of awareness and skills development activities alongside your actual improvement programme. This will raise the average Lean Healthcare skill level available to the organisation.

Warning sign 7: *Communication melt-down*

What you will experience

This is one that comes on quite slowly as people stop turning up to event briefings, progress meetings or improvement groups. You start to feel that things are going on behind your back or things are not happening and you are having difficulty finding out why. Meetings will be cancelled with increasing frequency and the flow of information coming from teams will slow to a trickle or will stop.

Why it happens

This happens when leaders start to disengage but it is also often driven by the behaviour of practitioners themselves. For example they might be repeatedly chasing for information from the front-line team who do not understand why it is required, holding meetings with no purpose, or simply having a complex structure for your improvement programme.

What you can do about it

Review the information you genuinely want to gather (refer back to your scoping session) and also to the structure you have established for your Lean Healthcare programme.

Ensure that your meetings run to time and have a defined problem to solve (rather than simply being lengthy progress reviews).

Warning sign 8: *Next new 'fad' launched*

What you will experience

You are in the middle of your Lean Healthcare Programme when you receive an unexpected email from the CEO announcing a new improvement initiative that does not seem to fit with the Lean Healthcare programme. When you talk to the CEO about it you are told that whilst Lean is important to the organisation, this new 'fad' will operate at a much more strategic level, or will have a different focus (for example more about patient safety than patient experience). Does this sound familiar?

Why it happens

This occurs because of a lack of understanding (sadly) by the management team about how to do Lean, or a perception that it is simply a tactical issue. You may also find that the new 'fad' is driven by a management consultancy being engaged by the organisation who has realised that whilst you are doing Lean they will need to convince the organisation to buy Product X as any attempt by them to sell Lean will get rebuffed with the statement, "We have Lean under control, thanks."

What you can do about it

Some of this is difficult to retrieve if you have not started out in the right place by ensuring that your improvement sponsor (who needs to be at Board level) truly promotes the Lean Healthcare programme as vital to the strategic direction of the organisation, and not just as a tactical 'Band-Aid'! If this happens when you are into the programme you will need to backtrack and ensure that your management team is aware of the strategic importance/impact of your Lean Healthcare programme. You will probably have to fight to ensure the programme is integrated into the new 'fad' rather than sidelined by it (or worse, made subservient to it!)

Warning sign 9:

Words & deeds not in alignment

What you will experience

Your managers and improvement sponsor will profess to support the programme and its strategic importance to the organisation but they fail to release resources (especially people), turn up for event briefings, allow minor expenditure etc. There will be other signs, normally body language and behaviours that do not support what they are saying.

Why it happens

This is caused by a myriad of reasons, often external to you and the organisation (such as new external pressures from an SHA etc). It can also be caused by discord in the management team. For example, where the CEO is passionate about the Lean Healthcare programme and pushes others on the board to support it, often against their will. Those objecting will often not be in a position to complain openly so have to say things that appear to support the programme but their behaviour will give them away.

There is an old saying relevant to this:

"What I believe affects how I behave

How I behave affects how the situation becomes

And if I believe it will fail, I will behave as if it will fail and, of course, it will fail."

What you can do about it

This is an issue for the improvement sponsor to sort out for you and may involve briefings with the leadership team to gain their commitment. You will probably also have to spend time with individual members of the board and influential senior clinicians to convince them of the importance of your Lean Healthcare programme.

Warning sign 10:

Moving from achievement to chatting

What you will experience

Your Lean events suddenly become 'Lean reviews' or Lean meetings and instead of delivering improvements and tangible changes they start to deliver lists of actions and lots of debate and arguments. Alternatively, after your actual Rapid Improvement Events or similar Lean events you install weekly progress meetings (a good thing) but within a week they become chat shops about why things were better before and why things can't move forward.

Why it happens

This is often caused by a lack of focus on a 'problem'. Give a team a challenge and many will rise up to it (for example; reduce length of stay, improve orthopaedic throughput or reduce the number of A&E presentations). Give the same team the objective of just making further improvements and there is nothing specific for them to aim at! Continuous Improvement teams work best when they are tackling specific problems – think of the most successful programmes you have been involved in and they will almost certainly be based around a problem, rather than a general improvement strategy.

What you can do about it

Never leave a team without a problem. When you have implemented some improvements you need to task the team with solving a new problem such as making the area 15% better or reducing the number of items on the risk register by five.

When you are establishing a new team give them a series of objectives that are achievable and measurable and make sure they remain focused on them!

Chapter summary

This chapter focused on listing the top ten warning signs that your Lean Healthcare programme may experience. The aim is to provide you with an early warning system that your programme is going off track and the chance to put it back on track.

Many of the top ten warning signs are interdependent (for example, loss of leadership interest will affect/create other warning signs) but we have tried to provide a spread of activity to give you the best chance of spotting problems early on so you can nip the problem in the bud. The top ten warning signs are summarised as:

1. Loss of leadership Interest
2. Loss of team input
3. Rolling roadblock
4. Silly season
5. No sustainability
6. Where has all the knowledge gone?
7. Communication melt-down
8. Next new 'fad' launched
9. Words & deeds not in alignment
10. Moving from achievement to chatting

This is not a definitive list and we would welcome details of your experiences. Just email us with your comments/ experience to *sustain@amnis-uk.com*.

5: Creating a Lean Healthcare organisation

Introduction

This chapter sets out a template that will ensure you are able to become a Lean Healthcare organisation. It brings together much of the thinking from earlier chapters and also introduces some new concepts to help you plan for, implement and sustain a Lean Healthcare organisation.

A Lean Healthcare organisation is one that:

1. Sees safety as paramount. No change will be considered unless it has been proven to deliver the process improvement in a safe manner to patients, staff and other people affected by it

2. Is seeing a 30% or more improvement year on year across a range of measures

3. Has an organisational culture that supports on-going improvement and innovation

4. Uses the best in Lean thinking practice, especially focusing on the 5 principles (Value, Value Stream, Flow, Pull & Continuous Improvement) **AND** other approaches (Six Sigma, Theory of Constraints etc) as appropriate

5. Has strength in depth in its ability to plan for, implement and sustain improvement
6. Has the support of clinicians, managers and front-line staff at all levels
7. Is recognised as a leader in the area of 'Lean Thinking' in Healthcare

This chapter remains relevant even if the aspiration to become a Lean Healthcare organisation is far beyond what you are trying to achieve. Why? Because even if you just want to use Lean to improve a few pathways and reduce the costs associated with them (whilst also improving patient safety and experience) you would still be wise to think about implementing a structure that supports long-term improvement. Otherwise you will end up with improvements that dissipate when the last Lean event ends.

Where are you going (and why)?

Before you even contemplate starting up a Lean Healthcare programme, you need to be very clear about where you going (in terms of what you want to achieve) and why you (or the organisation) want to go there! You also need to be realistic about the timescales and the time investment required to be successful. This does not mean you will need to wait for three years to achieve anything, but it does mean you should be thinking about committing your organisation to a journey measured in years (if you want to be a Lean Healthcare organisation) or at least months (for you to deliver sustainable improvements through your Lean Healthcare programme). Prior to doing anything, we would urge you to undertake a Scoping Session and we have provided an example guide of how to run one of these events in the Appendices.

Setting up the structure for success

In this section we explore the key structures you need to put in place if you want to create a Lean Healthcare organisation (or which you should be considering even if you just want to improve a few areas and pathways):

Improvement Group or Board

An Improvement Group is a cross-functional management team focused on supporting and furthering the aims of your Lean Healthcare programme and ensuring it is integrated with any other programmes of improvement being undertaken within your organisation. The Improvement Group is ideally chaired by your improvement sponsor (a board level champion) and should have representation from across the organisation, including senior clinicians, front-line staff and managers at various levels.

The Improvement Group is the mouthpiece of your Lean Healthcare programme at the main board meetings and also represents the Trust management at the closing briefs for your Lean events.

Develop the internal team

Sustainability is based on having a sufficient number of people trained to plan, implement and lead improvement events. Without this broad base of skills you are at risk of it being derailed if one or two key people leave the organisation.

Recommended percentages of people at various levels at the end of the first year should be:

- **Change agents (service improvement professionals)** – a minimum of three but ideally many more!
- **Practitioners** – Minimum of 5% (but ideally 8% or more)
- **Users:** 30–40%
- **The Aware** – Everyone else

These groups were referred to in more detail later in the book.

Raising & maintaining awareness

From the moment you announce that you are 'going Lean' you will need to focus on raising the awareness of your team as to what this actually means and then maintain that awareness through on-going update training sessions. Without this you will encounter increased resistance and lose out on the benefits from the improvements resulting from the ideas of your team.

Communication structure

Supporting your awareness programme (which is best done as a series of workshops and updates), you will also need to implement a communications structure. This is normally best done through a variety of media including emails, newsletters, staff briefings, open forums etc – a mix of approaches will ensure that everyone gets the message – but you will need to be consistent!

In addition to your communication structure, consider having communication 'pit stops' where staff (and visitors) can drop in and see pictures of 'before and after' and also read the results of what has been achieved. It should also contain details of future objectives for your Lean Healthcare programme and a celebration of the successes you are having (and what people have done!)

Continuous/focused improvement teams

Supporting your Lean events (such as Rapid Improvement Events, Value Stream Analysis Events, Rapid Planning Events etc) you need to establish a continuous improvement culture, both within the areas you are focusing on and generally around the organisation (at least until all areas have been touched by the process). This does not mean you need to get people together for an hour at a time once a week until it runs out of steam. You should **always** make sure the teams are focused; you can achieve this by getting them to tackle specific problems or to make specific improvements in one or more performance metrics. This is because if you ask people just to improve, you will achieve nothing!

After Lean events, the teams should be focusing on daily Improvements – a key Lean concept and closely related to continuous improvement but also including making sure that any old (and/or bad) habits do not creep back in!

Rapid response team

You will need to acknowledge that things will go wrong sometimes. Just learn from it and move forward. In the first year you should expect your programme to make two paces forward and one step back, but gradually the forward steps will increase and the backward steps decrease. However, it is also important for you to establish a rapid response process to deal with problems as you encounter them. For example, a mechanism for reporting any real roadblocks that your team encounter along with a process for getting rid of them (or answering them) within 24 hours. This helps keep you moving forward, but at the same time prevents snipers from doing rolling roadblocks.

What are you aiming for?

However far you want to go, your organisation may not be ready to follow you (or your management team may not want it to go that far!) Your organisation's culture may resist it (with culture being summarised as 'the way things are done around here!')

Lean purists talk about 'True North', the aim of constantly improving towards your organisation's real goals – which can only be defined in discussion with your organisations' stakeholders including your staff.

The success of your organisation is unlikely to be dependent on just your own department. Therefore it is up to you to determine where you want to go and why.

How long will it take?

If you are set on becoming a Lean Healthcare organisation it will take you at least three years and possibly more and the journey will go something like that outlined in the table overleaf.

Chapter summary

In this chapter we have outlined the key things you need to consider if you want to become a Lean Healthcare organisation and these include:

1. Establishing an Improvement Group/Board
2. Developing your Internal Team
3. Raising & Maintaining Awareness
4. Setting up a Communications Structure
5. Establish Continuous/Focused Improvement Team
6. Put in place a Rapid Response Process

But, above all you want to clear about where you are going and why, as well as being realistic about how long it takes to get there! You need to create a compelling vision or image of what the end state looks like and the resulting benefits. This will keep motivation levels high and engage people's hearts as well as their minds.

	Year 1	Year 2	Year 3
Skills	• Service improvement team established • First practitioners developed • Lots of awareness events	• Service improvement team now effective • Practitioners taking on the role as pseudo-Service improvement team • Everyone has participated in a Lean event or workshop	• Practitioners and service improvement team almost interchangeable • All staff have been involved in one or more Lean events
Activities	• First redesign events *(VSE)* • First Rapid Improvement Events – around 30% of which will have problems	• Focus on embedding changes and continuous improvement • Fewer *'Rapid Improvement Events'* and more engagement with external stakeholders occurring	• Appropriate use of fast and slow approaches *(fast being Rapid Improvement Events and slow being continuous improvement teams)* • Projects being tackled effectively
Noise	• Snipers quite active and lots of noise generated • First positive case studies	• Noise reaches a peak as Snipers realise the changes are here to stay • Your advocates and positives are now becoming a force to be reckoned with	• Snipers either leave or go quiet • Over-whelming positive noise

Structure	• Fluid structure – with variable amounts of management involvement	• Rigid structure as it is realised that looser structures do not work	• Semi-fluid structure possible as the organisational culture shifts for good!
Learning	• Poor knowledge sharing structures	• Strong knowledge sharing systems in place *(including NVQs and eLearning opportunities)*	• Informal knowledge sharing *(round the coffee machine)* and via Communication Pit Stops.
Pace of Change	• Medium to slow	• Medium to Fast	• Medium

6: Four key checklists

Introduction

In this chapter we will summarise some of the key aspects of sustainability and the journey you will embark upon during your Lean Healthcare programme as you work towards becoming a Lean Healthcare organisation. Some of these topics have been covered elsewhere in this book and for these this section should act as a summary. Where the topics are new, this section summarises the key issues and points you in the right direction for further study.

This chapter is called 'four key checklists' for the simple reason that it consists of the following four checklists:

1. **The Success Checklist** – a summary of the top ten things that will differentiate your Lean Healthcare programme from all the ones that fail.
2. **The People Checklist** – a summary of the different types of people you will encounter on the journey.
3. **The Tools Checklist** – a summary of the top ten tools that support sustainable improvement.

4. **The Culture Checklist** – a quick overview of how your organisation's culture is shaped and how it can affect the success of your improvement programme.

The Success Checklist

This checklist summarises the top ten things that differentiate a successful Lean Healthcare programme from one that will not live up to its potential:

1. **An Improvement Board/group** – a cross-functional team with senior support (both managerial and clinical) which coordinates all improvement activities, overcomes roadblocks and sets the pace of change.
2. **Service Improvement team** – a team of change agents with the expertise to lead a variety of Lean events and activities, such as Pathway Redesign Events (VSEs) and Rapid Improvement Events (RIEs).
3. **Communication structure** – an organised structure of communications, awareness workshops and knowledge sharing activities that provides your team with the opportunity to learn, to input and to share best practice.
4. **End to end focus** – looking at all activities end to end rather than picking isolated areas for improvement and involving representatives from all areas/teams involved.
5. **Roadblock demolition** – a process for dealing with roadblocks and problems that happen quickly.
6. **Being problem focused** – ensuring that teams are problem focused and always have something to tackle – rather than following off in an unstructured 'let's improve everything' approach.
7. **Removing the 'old shoes'** – taking away the ability of the teams to make mistakes and slip back into bad habits.

8. **Accepting occasional failure & celebrating success** – accepting that not everything will work first time and learning from mistakes, as well as ensuring that successes are celebrated and the knowledge shared.

9. **Accepting resistance** – accepting that some people will be 'anti' the Lean Healthcare programme for a variety of reasons. Some will have genuine concerns and will need to be listened to, others will need more information to bring them round and, lastly, some will just not want to play and will need to be sidelined.

10. **Walking the boards & the wards** – ensuring active management input into the process to ensure that improvements stick and old habits do not creep back in. It is also important to congratulate those involved and demonstrate that the management structure really do care about long term improvements through your Lean Healthcare programme and not just quick fixes.

The People Checklist

The following is a checklist of the types of people your organisation has (as well as the types of people you will need to make sure you put in place):

The people you will have met

The following are a list of the types of people you will encounter in your organisation irrespective of where you are on your Lean Healthcare journey.

- **Advocates** – people who will be very positive about the need for change and will sing the praises of your Lean Healthcare programme. If you can find clinical advocates that's even better!

- **Positives** – people who will be positive about the programme and will actively participate. The difference between Advocates and Positives is that positives will actively engage in your Lean Healthcare programme but will not shout about it.
- **Neutrals** – people who will be undecided about the programme, being neither negative nor positive about it. They are waiting to find out how it all goes.
- **Negatives** – people who are against the programme and show their displeasure at being involved through negative body language, finding roadblocks to the programme and always having an excuse for something not to be done.
- **Snipers** – people who are actively against the programme and who go out of their way to encourage others to disconnect from your Lean Healthcare programme. Snipers can be very clever and are motivated by a variety of reasons. Some can be turned around; others will need to be sidelined. The difference between a Sniper and a Negative is the fact that a Sniper will actively go out of their way to disrupt and stall the programme and will encourage others not to participate, whereas a Negative just does not want to be involved, but does not actively stop others participating.
- **Influencers** – people who have the ability to sway the opinion of others. Influencers are at the bottom of this list because they can come from any of the other categories – you can have very influential Snipers as well as influential Advocates. Finding the influencers in your programme and ensuring they are on-side is essential to your success! Influencers can be at any level in the organisation – it is their unofficial position as an influencer of the opinion of others rather than their job title that counts!

The people you will need to put in place

The following are a list of the various roles that will be essential to the success of your Lean Healthcare programme:

- **Improvement sponsor** – a board level champion of your Lean Healthcare programme, who genuinely cares about the programme, believes in its importance and is prepared to advocate for you at board meetings.
- **Change agents** – your service improvement specialists who will facilitate improvements but will not be responsible for the improvements themselves – that is the role of the people in the teams at the front-line.
- **Practitioners** – people with the ability to lead events, but who also have a day job. These people are often assistant managers or managers of areas and are responsible for initiating improvements when they spot problems.
- **Team leaders** – individuals who are appointed to run Lean events, meaning they are there for the full programme of activity, coordinate the efforts of the group and also ensure that the objectives of the event are met. A guide for team leaders is provided in the Appendices.
- **Users** – a large group of people that will, after a time, have participated in a Lean event of some form and who understand the key principles.
- **The Aware** – the remainder of the organisation who are none of the above, but who need to be aware of the Lean Healthcare programme, its aims and how they can contribute. As time goes on the people in this group will move into one of the other groups (users, practitioners or change agents) until eventually there is no-one in this group!

The Tools Checklist

In this checklist we outline some of the key tools that support a sustainable Lean Healthcare programme. Some of this section is repeated from our original book *Lean for Practitioners*, but we have highlighted the tools that best support sustainable improvement and how it can help. For more detailed information please refer to our *Lean for Practitioners* book, a copy of which can be obtained by signing up to our newsletter group from *www.amnis-uk.com*

$5S^{+1}$

$5S^{+1}$ is a process designed to create a visual workplace, which is somewhere that is organised with safety in mind and which conforms to the *5 Second Rule* in that it is obvious to an informed person what is going on within 5 Seconds of them entering the area. It is sometimes called 5S but we have modified the original 5S terms to add a ($^{+1}$) of Safety, as decisions in Healthcare in particular need to be measured against the impact on patient safety. Some people confuse this activity with a tidy up but in fact $5S^{+1}$ is a systematic way of managing a process to reduce the effort required to run the process and the risk to staff and customers.

The steps involved in undertaking a $5S^{+1}$ exercise are outlined below:

- **Sort** – remove unwanted items from the area to reduce clutter
- **Set** – set what remains in order and give each item a marked 'home location'
- **Shine** – keep the area clean and take all items to their marked home location at the ends of shifts/clinics

- **Standardise** – put in place protocols that define the team responsibilities for managing the process
- **Sustain** – audit and improve the area
- **Safety** ($^{+1}$) – at each step, ensure you are not making decisions detrimental to patient or staff safety

An example $5S^{+1}$ Audit form can be found in the Appendices and it helps people to continuously improve their area by focusing on specific problems related to creating visual controls. To support sustainable improvement we would recommend doing a regular (meaning at least three times per week) $5S^{+1}$ audit for the first four weeks following a Lean event.

Standard work

At its simplest, *Standard Work* is simply a method of ensuring that everyone involved in delivering a process uses the same or similar processes. Standard work can be a specialised activity and may need specialised help to do it fully, but in its simplest form it consists of straightforward guides showing how to run a process including:

- **Method Sheets** – used to outline how a process is undertaken
- **Layout Sheets** – used to demonstrate how an area is 'laid out'
- **Loading Charts** – used to calculate the staffing required for an area
- **Key Points Sheet** – used to highlight specific weaknesses/ areas to watch for in a process

Standard work supports a sustainable Lean Healthcare programme by getting consistency in the way things are done. It helps reduce the time taken for people joining the team to get up to speed and decreases the chance that they will bring in bad habits, as well as maximizing the effectiveness of the team.

FMEA

FMEA (Failure Modes & Effects Analysis) creates a priority list for addressing risks in a process by multiplying level of risk.

FMEA supports a Sustainable Lean Healthcare Programme by reducing the possibility of introducing any additional Patient Safety Risks as a result of the Lean improvements. It also provides a focus for Continuous/Focused Improvement Teams to continue to improve by eliminating any outstanding risks identified through FMEA.

5 Whys (Root Cause Analysis)

5 Whys is a simple tool used to help identify the root cause of a problem. It relies on asking the question 'Why' five times, with the idea being that the root cause will be exposed by the time of the fifth question as we have tried to show below:

Problem: Patient not called as promised

Why 1 – Why did the Patient not get called back?

Answer: *Because they were not on the 'to call' list*

Why 2 – Why did their name not appear on the 'to call' list?

Answer: *Because their details were not in the 'to call' folder*

Why 3 – Why were their details not in the folder?

Answer: *Because the standard form was not completed to say they should be there*

Why 4 – Why was the standard form not used?

Answer: *Because 'X' has only recently joined the team and did not know the process*

Why 5 – Why did we not induct 'X' correctly? (Root Cause)

Root Cause Analysis supports a Sustainable Lean Healthcare programme by getting people not to respond to the symptoms of a problem but to eliminate it for good.

SPC (Statistical Process Control)

SPC is a tool frequently used in Lean and Six Sigma projects to monitor the performance of a process to measure variance and to spot trends that could indicate a problem or dangerous activity prior to it occurring. SPC supports a Sustainable Lean Healthcare programme by providing a warning that a process is going out of control before it gets 'too bad'.

Fishbone diagrams (Ishikawa diagrams)

Fishbone diagrams, (also known as cause & effect diagrams) are creative tools used to identify the primary causes of a problem (effect).

Fishbone diagrams supports a Sustainable Lean Healthcare programme by helping people to explore the causes of a problem/symptom and structuring a process for improvement.

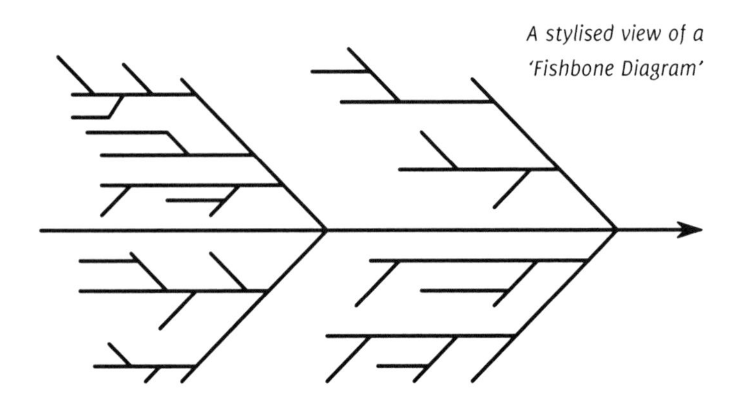

A stylised view of a 'Fishbone Diagram'

The Culture Change Checklist

An organisation's culture is the result of a number of influences that are illustrated in the diagram below:

As culture is difficult to create on purpose, many people believe, mistakenly, that you cannot directly change an organisation's culture. However, there are specific factors that directly and indirectly affect the culture of an organisation (depicted by the circle in the centre of the model). The difficulty lies in aligning each of the influences so that the culture that emerges is the one that you want.

If you think of an organisation's culture as simply "the way things happen" then the first step in culture development is to define how you want things to happen in the future. For example, do you want the organisation to be "creative" or "patient focused"? Once this is clear, the culture change programme is assembled rather like a jigsaw, with four main areas:

1. Leadership (define the vision, agree performance framework, model behaviour)
2. Management (drive change, set goals, operate systems)
3. Systems (IT, HR policies & procedures, facilities)
4. People (commitment, team working, flexibility)

A change in any one of these four areas will change your organisation's culture for better or worse.

The checklist overleaf will enable you to assess the scope of the culture change programme that lies before you.

Component	Rating Not at All ——————————————— Completely 1 — — — — — 5 — — — — — 10
The target culture is clearly defined	
Leaders model the required behaviour	
Managers drive the changes	
Systems support the target culture	
People are committed to the vision	
The project is adequately resourced	
The patients understand our vision	

Chapter Summary

This chapter has been concerned with providing you with four essential checklists to help your organisation, including:

- **The Success Checklist** – a checklist of the top ten things that differentiate success from failure in Lean Healthcare programmes.
- **The People Checklist** – a checklist of the types of people you will meet on your Lean Healthcare journey and the ones you will need to put in place.
- **The Tools Checklist** – a checklist of the top tools for sustaining improvement (plus a checklist of the tools used at key stages in the Lean Healthcare process).
- **The Culture Change Checklist** – a quick review of how you shape organisational culture and a quick checklist to estimate the scale of the culture change your organization will need to undertake.

Obviously, we have only touched the surface on the organisational culture strand and we would be happy to provide you with further information should you require it, and to answer your questions, just email us at *sustain@amnis-uk.com.*

7: The next eight things to do...

Introduction

Who would have thought we would have arrived at the last chapter so quickly! Well, after this chapter the reins are being handed over to you (although we would be happy to answer your additional questions – just email *sustain@amnis-uk.com*). As a final piece of advice we have summarised the next eight things we believe you should be doing with your Lean Healthcare programme. Then you just need to look through the appendices and work it all out for yourself – but you know you are capable of it!

1. Review where you are now

Be clear about the legacy you are carrying from earlier programmes before you start the journey. Also, make sure you really do have a problem to solve, as without a clear 'pain' in your organisation to be fixed you are doomed to failure. Indeed, the bigger and clearer everyone can see (and 'feel') the pain your organisation is suffering from, the easier it will be to be successful!

A summary questionnaire for you to use to assess your organisation against the CRITICAL areas of success we explored earlier in this book is provided in the Appendices.

2. Set out your roadmap

Having assessed where you are (and worked out how to tackle any residual resistance you might encounter), you should set out your plan of where you personally want to get to with your Lean Healthcare programme. Is it just a 'Band-Aid' on a particular problem, or an organisation wide change? It does not matter what your ambitions are, but you need to be clear about what you want before you start.

3. Engage your leaders & managers

It is essential to the long-term success of your Lean Healthcare programme that your managers and leaders are engaged in the process and care for it as much as you do! Set up your improvement group and ask managers and leaders to participate (along with a broad spectrum of other people from across the organisation) and ensure they turn up to the opening & closing briefs for Lean events.

4. Create your organisation's Lean Healthcare vision

Having worked out your own personal vision of success in Step 2, you need to create a consolidated vision for your organisation with the support of your managers and leaders, and based on the feedback from others in your improvement group. Once you have it, you need to share the vision with the rest of the organisation!

5. Scope a programme (and have a go!)

Having taken the plunge and created your vision, the next step is to scope a programme! Find one that is a real problem that people recognise so they will understand why it has been chosen (or work hard to let them know why it has been taken). Also, pick your first project to meet the following three criteria:

1. It must be easily achievable in three to five months
2. It must have easily targeted 'wins' that you are confident can be achieved
3. It must be something people believe needs to be improved

A guide to running a scoping session is found in the Appendices.

6. Move from discussion into action!

Having scoped the programme, don't get stuck in discussion mode – go on and redesign a pathway (or at the very least implement a Rapid Improvement Event of some kind). You will find a checklist of how to organise a Lean event in the Appendices as well as a guide of how to run a Pathway Redesign Exercise (VSE).

7. Be insistent (and demanding)

Having started to make improvements you will encounter your first significant resistance both verbally (in terms of roadblocks) but also in terms of inaction and you will need to be insistent that things are done. This is where your well-organised improvement group becomes invaluable!

8. Celebrate your first successes

Celebrate every success and ensure the learning that has been gained is shared and used again. You should also capture positive feedback from your front-line teams so they can be used to inspire others to take part!

Chapter summary

As we reach the end of this book, this chapter has focused on the next eight steps you should be thinking about taking in your attempts to create a sustainable, safe and responsible Lean Healthcare programme. These are summarised as:

1. Review where you are now
2. Set out your roadmap
3. Engage your leaders & managers
4. Create your organisation's Lean Healthcare vision
5. Scope a programme (and have a go!)
6. Move from discussion into action
7. Be insistent (and demanding)
8. Celebrate your first successes

Whatever you choose to do, make sure you enjoy it – Lean Healthcare programmes should be fun as well as beneficial to your organisation!

Let us know how you get on – just email us at *sustain@amnis-uk.com.*

About the Authors

Mark Eaton *MSc MBA CEng FRSA*

Mark is a Chartered Engineer and has been involved in leading Lean transformations for over ten years. Formerly the director of the DTI's Flagship Lean Transformation programme for Manufacturing in a number of UK regions, Mark has subsequently branched out into delivering Lean in the NHS, Armed Forces and the wider Public Sector.

Mark is Chair of the IET's Manufacturing Network and a member of their Healthcare Executive Team.

Mark was awarded the Viscount Nuffield Medal in 2004 for his contribution to UK Industry.

Simon Phillips *MA FRSA*

Simon has been involved in helping others prepare for, organise and lead change all his professional life. His first book on personal effectiveness, published by McGraw Hill, was an Amazon bestseller and sold in 16 countries worldwide.

Simon's career began as a Change consultant with Andersen Consulting (now Accenture). Responsible for leading large change projects across many sectors, he established himself as both an accomplished consultant and a thought-leader, particularly in the areas of training, communication and culture change.

Simon is a frequent contributor to seminars, conferences and workshops on culture change and new ways of working. Together with Mark, he is the co-leader of Europe's largest network of independent consultants, trainers and coaches and he won a National Training Award in 2006.

Appendix 1
Key Lean phrases & concepts

Lean events

RIE:	Rapid Improvement Event (RIE) – a structured way of implementing tangible improvements.
RPE:	Rapid Planning Event (RPE) – a structured process to de-risk a critical process prior to an RIE
VSE:	Value Stream Analysis Event (VSE) – a process to re-design 1 or more key Pathways
CAD:	Change Agent Development (CAD) – a programme to develop internal change agents
FIT:	Focused Improvement Teams (FIT) – groups focused on a specific issue or continuous improvement

Scoping Session: A process to set the boundaries, expectations, objectives, roles and timing for change to occur

Change roles

Improvement Sponsor (IS) – a board level representative who champions change

Pathway or Process Owner (PO) – the specific manager/ director who owns each process being transformed

Change Agent (CA) – an internal specialist in change who leads on-going improvements

Team Leader (TL) – the person leading a VSE, RIE, RPE or other Lean event

Specific tools

In addition to standard Lean, Six Sigma or similar tools, the following are a list of tools and concepts used specifically by Amnis:

Diverge/Converge: A creative tool that is used to explore problems and then group them for action

Design 5: A creative tool that involves designing 5 different solutions to a problem

D&P: Design & plan (D&P) – a creative process used as part of an RPE

DMT:	Design, move & test (DMT) – a process to create, implement and prove a new layout during a RIE
Beauty Competition:	A rational scoring process to select one of the solutions designed by Design 5
Try It:	Physically going to an area and testing that a new process will work/fit
Test It:	The same as 'Try It', used for information based processes
Paper Layout:	A scale plan of an area showing how an area will be laid out
Corporate Project:	An improvement activity too big to be undertaken during a Lean event
Do It:	A simple action that can be undertaken with little or no management input
Process Facts:	Key facts relating to a process being improved
Hand-off Charts:	A diagram showing how information and people are handed off through a process

20+ improvements:	A creative process designed to identify 20 or more improvements to a current process
Data at a glance:	A summary of key process data which is used as a business dashboard
Opening brief:	A brief given at the start of a VSE, RIE or RPE to set the scope and objectives for an event
Closing brief:	A brief given by the team at the end of a VSE, RIE or RPE to summarise achievements

The Five Lean Principles

Value	understand the things that add value to the customer
Value Stream	understand how that value is delivered
Flow	eliminate bottlenecks and help the value 'flow'
Pull	trigger activity on demand
Continuous Improvement	create a culture of continuous improvement and review

Key Lean concepts & terminology

Runners:	An activity that occurs regularly and runs every day (or equivalent)
Repeater:	An activity that occurs frequently, but maybe not every day, i.e. appears monthly
Stranger:	An activity that occurs now and again i.e. appears once per year
Planned work:	Work that can be scheduled and planned for
Emergent work:	Work that arises during the process (i.e. unseen problems & unexpected activities)
Value:	An activity that increases the worth of a product or service to the customer
Waste:	An activity that adds cost but which does not increase value (in the eyes of the customer)
WORMPIT:	The acronym for the seven Wastes found in all processes
Value stream:	The steps involved in delivering value to the end customer

Takt time: The beat rate of an area calculated as demand rate/ available time

Lead time: The total time taken from start to finish

Process time: The actual 'touch time' spent working on the job

Pull: The concept of only doing something when the customer demands it (see also Kanban)

Flow: A process flows when there are no delays or bottlenecks and it delivers consistently

1 Piece Flow: The concept of only moving one item at a time

Bullwhip: The effect of a small change at one end of a process causing a big change downstream

Standard work: A series of tools to control how people undertake a process so that it is repeatable

Kanban: A system that controls the availability of parts via visual triggers (aka Pull system)

Supermarket:	Similar to a Kanban, a stock of items/information which is used to service an area
E2E:	End to end – the ability to look at a process from the start to the end
Visual management:	The '5 Second Rule' i.e. I can see what is going on in five seconds
$5S^{+1}$:	A tool to create and sustain a visually managed work area safely
SMED:	Single Minute Exchange of Die (SMED) – a process to shorten change-over times

Appendix 2: $5S^{+1}$ Audit Form *sheet 1*

Area	Check Question	0	1	2	3	4	5
Sort	Are there unneeded items in the area?						
	Is there equipment or other materials that are being held but not used?						
	Are there any unused documentation or instruments in the area?						
Score: ______	Is it obvious which items are current and in use?						
Set	Is it obvious what happens in the work areas and are control processes in place?						
	Are signs for storage places for documents and equipment in place and correct?						
	Are all shelved and stored items labelled and located correctly?						
Score: ______	Are the purposes of different areas clearly marked and are they correct?						
Shine	Are the work area and floors kept free of clutter and tidy?						
	Are items returned to their 'home' locations at the end of every working day or shift?						
	Are the required equipment and materials available and in good working order?						
Score: ______	Do employees know their $5S^{+1}$ routine?						

Appendix 2: $5S^{+1}$ Audit Form *sheet 2*

Standardise

Does everyone understand the purpose of their $5S^{+1}$ activities?

Is there a maintenance standard or checklist for each process or piece of equipment?

Is there a clear improvement plan for each area?

Are there clear instructions visible for how to operate the area's $5S^{+1}$ process?

Score: ________

Sustain

Do employees implement the $5S^{+1}$ criteria consistently?

Is there a regular audit schedule to monitor $5S^{+1}$ performance?

Does the area leader take an active interest in $5S^{+1}$ and the actions arising?

Do employees & managers take action to correct low scores on the $5S^{+1}$ Audit?

Score: ________

Safety

Has a risk assessment been undertaken and actioned?

Are required safety procedures available and in place?

Is there an on-going programme to look at and reduce risks in the area?

Are the team aware of how their role contributes to managing and reducing risk?

Score: ________

Scoring levels: *5* = Exceptional – no room for improvement • *4* = Very good / could be used as best practice example
3 = Good requirements exceeded in some areas • *2* = Acceptable / requirements met
1 = More effort required to make improvements • *0* = No improvement made or no evidence available

Appendix 3

How to do Lean really, really badly – a modern parable

Sunday morning 9am

There is an article in the Sunday Times about the use of 'Lean in Healthcare' – and the scissors are used on it!

Monday morning 9am

An email is sent to the senior managers that the organisation will be 'going Lean'

Tuesday morning 9am

A management meeting where the 'Lean Team' are appointed from amongst a group of harassed and busy nurses and managers

Wednesday morning 9am

The first 'Lean Team Meeting', sadly none of the management team are free to attend

Thursday morning 9am

The 'Lean Team Leader' decides that this Lean thing is a bit too much trouble and 'goes back to their day job.

Friday morning 9am

A management crisis meeting is held to review the reasons why 'Lean' has failed to deliver

Saturday morning 9am

Much scratching of heads whilst they cut the grass about why their investment in Lean did not deliver

Sunday morning 9am

There is an article in the Sunday Times about using the 'Theory of Constraints' to save Healthcare

Monday morning 9am

Lean is dead! Long live the Theory of Constraints!

Appendix 4

Guide to common sayings

This Appendix is designed to be slightly humorous but with a serious message. In your journey toward Lean you will meet lots of people; some will be advocates (or positives) for the changes, some will be neutral (not really concerned either way) and some will be negatives.

At the start of the change process it will be difficult to spot the difference between the neutrals (who will ask lots of awkward questions because they want to understand why something is happening) and the negatives (who will ask awkward questions because they want to find reasons or ammunition to make the change fail).

The following is a short summary of some of the key phrases you will hear from people and our suggestion of what they are really saying...

What is said	What is meant
"This won't work here."	"I don't want this to work"
"Lean isn't applicable to our environment."	"I don't know what Lean really is."
"I don't have the time."	"This is not important enough."
"I hear what you are saying."	"...and I am going to ignore it."
"I will have a go but I think it will fail."	"It will fail."
"The team don't really want to do this."	"I don't really want to do this."
"We are already Lean and cut to the bone."	"I don't know what Lean really is."
"5S[+1] does not apply here."	"I don't want to do this."
"I can't see the benefit of visual management."	"I don't want people to see how we work here."
"Lean is just like process mapping."	"I really don't understand what Lean is."
"It will get done sometime."	"It will never get done."
"We can pick it up next time."	"...by which time you'll have forgotten about it."
"I can't give you a timescale."	"...because I don't want to be held to it."
"I think batching jobs is more efficient."	"I don't understand the impact on customers."

Appendix 5

Example guide to how to run a scoping session

A scoping session lasts 3–4 hours and the outcome is an agreed plan (or Scoping Paper) that details what you are attempting to achieve through your programme for improvement. The plan is created by a group which ideally includes representatives from all areas affected and the resulting document should be widely communicated. Experience says that an effective Scoping Paper can double the probability that your programme will achieve the outcomes you are looking for. This short document sets out how to run a **scoping session.**

Prior to the scoping session	Complete
Agree attendee list with a minimum requirement being: • Project sponsor (Director) • Process owners (Area Managers affected) • Change agents (any internal improvement staff who will support the project)	
Gather background data	

Prepare an opening statement for the scoping session, which normally consists of:

- Stating what topic/issue or area needs improvement
- Why it is important to us (including any background information)
- What we would like to change and by when would we like it changed

Scoping session agenda

Agenda item	Description
Opening statement	Review opening statement created prior to the event
Open discussion	Deal with any questions or clarification requirements
Develop compelling need	Create an inspiring statement that details why this project must happen
Fix measures of success	Outline 3-5 critical measures of success for the programme
Identify scenarios	Outline scenarios which fully test the pathways to be improved
Outline who is in scope	Detail which areas (and individuals) are going to be involved FT/PT
Outline the fixed points	Outline the boundaries, risks and any thing which cannot be changed
Identify key roles	Identify the improvement sponsor & change agents
Set out your activity plan	Set out the plan for activities associated with the project
Fix your communications	Identify how the scoping paper will be communicated

After the scoping session	Complete
Complete the scoping paper and add in any missing detail	
Communicate the scoping paper	
Plan for the next steps in the programme	

Appendix 6

Example guide of how to run a VSE

A VSE (Value Stream Analysis Event) lasts for between 2 and 4 days and normally occurs after a 'Scoping Session' has happened. A VSE is used to first understand and then to redesign how an organisation delivers its services (and products if appropriate) in one or more critical areas. A Value Stream (also called a Pathway) is defined as all the steps involved in delivering services from one end to the other (from initial referral to patient discharge for example).

This document sets out how to run a **VSE.**

Prior to the VSE

4 weeks prior to VSE	Complete
Book the room, confirm attendees and plan for any disruption that will occur	
Identify and collect data to be collected prior to the event	
Create an event pack consisting of: • Post Its® • Clear tape • Masking tape • Blu-Tack® • Brown paper • Rubbish bags • Flipchart & pens,	
Agree that the improvement sponsor will deliver the opening brief	

3 weeks prior to VSE	Complete
Create opening brief which normally is drawn straight from the scoping paper	
Ask individuals in the areas affected to list what they believe are the top ten 'hurts'	
Confirm the expected benefits from the VSE	

2 weeks prior to VSE	Complete
Finalise opening brief	
Remind attendees about timings & venue	

1 week prior to VSE	Complete
Confirm all required data for event is available	

VSE agenda

Agenda	Description
Opening brief	Normally delivered by the improvement sponsor
Refresher training	Refresher training for all staff involved in the process
Current state	Identify how the process currently works using tools such as: • Process analysis (Mapping) • Hand-off charts • String diagrams • Data at a glance • Questions to be answered
Daily closing brief	Delivered every evening (except the day before the final closing brief): • What has been achieved today • What questions need to be answered • What we will be doing tomorrow

'Blue Sky' state	Create a without boundaries solution using: • Blue Sky diagrams • Concept capture sheets • Opening questioning
Future state	Create a realistic plan of how the process will work in 6-12 months time: • Future state map • Implementation plan • Benefits summary • Revised layouts • Questions still to be answered
Closing brief	Delivered by the team, normally with the following agenda: • Welcome & overview of objectives • Review of the current state • Review of the Blue Sky state • Review of the future state • Review of the Implementation plan & benefits • Review of lessons learned • Questions

After the VSE	
1 week after the VSE	**Complete**
Communicate the results of the VSE	
Confirm the implementation plan and prepare for first events	
Ask team/s affected to identify how they will cope with the disruption of events	
Review all outstanding questions and obtain answers where possible	
2 weeks after the VSE	**Complete**
Undertake awareness briefings for all staff involved in first events	
Agree start-times and event duration for the first events	
Collect key process data, which often includes: • Activity data (what the staff do) • Volume (how often they do each activity) • Touch time (how much actual work is involved in doing each activity) • Lead time (how long it takes from the start to the end)	
Get each team involved in first improvement events to identify their top ten ‘hurts’	

3 weeks after the VSE	Complete
Identify other preparatory work the team/s affected could do which could include: • Detailed process mapping • Hand-off charts • String diagrams • Identification of improvement opportunities Remind attendees about timings & venue/s	

4 weeks after the VSE	Complete
Undertake first improvement events	

Appendix 7

Example responsibilities for Lean team leaders

What is a team leader?

A team leader is a person responsible for leading a team during an improvement event (such as a Value Stream Analysis Event or a Rapid Improvement Event). The team leader does not need to be a supervisor or manager but does need to work in, or have a good understanding of, the area under review and the people involved. The following is a summary of the responsibilities of team leaders at various phases of an event:

Responsibilities prior to the event

Prior to the Lean event the team leader will often work with the nominated change agents to assist in collecting data about the area, briefing the staff about what is occurring and also identifying the top ten 'hurts' for the area.

Responsibilities during the event

During the Lean event the team leader will support the smooth running of the event by helping the team to quickly reach consensus, by organising people within the group to undertake specific activities that need to be done (such as collecting further information etc) and by leading the daily closing brief (see below).

Responsibilities after the event

After the Lean event the team leader will continue to support the achieved improvements by helping to communicate the results of the event and also auditing improvements (where appropriate) to ensure that the new ways of working become part of the 'way things are done'.

Other team leader responsibilities

In addition to the outline of tasks detailed above the team leaders will sometimes also assist in organising the Lean events by booking rooms and organising the Lean event packs (which contain Post-Its®, Sellotape®, brown paper, etc).

Daily closing brief

(open to all people not directly involved in the event but who have an interest in it)

At the end of every day in all Lean events (except the last night of the event as the team will be doing an event closing brief), the Team Leader will organise (and will most often lead) a daily closing brief which has the following agenda:

- What we achieved today
- What the problems/questions are that we need answered
- What we are doing tomorrow

Appendix 8

Lean event checklist

The following is a checklist of the things to consider prior to any improvement event:

Complete	Action
	Are the objectives of the event clear?
	Are the timings of the event arranged?
	Has the team been selected for the event, including the Team Leader?
	Is the team ready to undertake the event (including coping with the time out)?
	Has everyone affected been told about what is going on even though they may not be involved directly in the improvement event?
	Has the base data relevant to the process been collected? (see below)
	Has a $5S^{+1}$ audit been undertaken to gather an initial score? (not for VSEs)
	Has the team identified their top ten 'hurts'?
	Have any relevant H&S or patient safety issues been discussed/reviewed and actioned?

	Is the event pack of materials available for the event (Post Its®, brown paper, tape etc)?
	Has someone been allocated to undertake the opening brief for the team?
	Is the team leader aware of Lean and their responsibilities in managing the team?
	Has any necessary training been undertaken?
	Are all required services in place for the event (IT support, equipment etc)?
	Has everyone who has an interest in the event been invited to the daily closing briefs?

Complete	Action
	Does everyone know the time for the team closing brief at the end of the event?
	Has anyone with a concern about the event had the opportunity to discuss what is going to happen with a change agent?
	Do you feel you have remembered everything that needs to be done?

Outline of event data

The following is a summary of the data that might need to be collected prior to an event:

- Frequency of occurrences/demand rate & changes expected in the future
- Lead time (total time from start to end of the process)
- Touch time (how much actual work is involved from start to end of the process)
- Failure rates, risks and/or associated patient incidents

Appendix 9
CRITICAL checklist

The **CRITICAL Diagnostic Lite (CDL)** is provided for clients who are either preparing for, implementing or attempting to sustain an improvement programme and is based on the much more comprehensive full CRITICAL Diagnostic.

The **CRITICAL Diagnostic Lite (CDL)** assists in the identification of weak spots within the organisation but does not offer a corrective action plan and as it is based on self-assessment the results may not be as robust as an independent review.

Method

The diagnostic should be given to a minimum of 3% of all people who are, or will be, involved in the improvement process from across all grades of staff, and ideally it will be given to greater than 5% of all staff affected. As a minimum, it needs to be given to one person from each grade of staff affected and also one person from each area affected by the improvement process.

The diagnostic consists of eight categories, with each category consisting of five questions. Each person completing the questionnaire must answer all 40 questions based on selecting a score between one and seven, where one indicates that the person completely disagrees with the statement, four indicates they neither agree of disagree with the statement and seven indicates that they completely agree with the statement.

The diagnostic coordinator should collate the results and the summary sheet completed (the last page of this document).

It is strongly advised that there is a strong communication about the purpose of undertaking the **CRITICAL Diagnostic Lite (CDL)**. It should stress how it will assist the organisation get the most from its improvement activities and that people should feel free to answer the questions as honestly as possible, without fear of any 'come back'. The results should be collated and reported anonymously to assist people to feel more comfortable about the process.

CRITICAL Diagnostic Lite (CDL)

Self-Assessment Form

This diagnostic has been provided to you to assist in helping us make the most of our improvement activities. Please answer all 40 questions by choosing a score of between 1 and 7 using the following scale:

1 = I completely disagree

2 = I strongly disagree

3 = I disagree slightly

4 = I neither agree nor disagree

5 = I agree slightly

6 = I strongly agree

7 = I completely agree

The questionnaire is based on the CRITICAL model, where each letter indicates one of the main reasons why an improvement programme (such as Lean, Six Sigma etc) might fail and stands for:

C = Communications

R = Resources

I = Involvement

T = Training

I = Implementation

C = Compass

A = Achievement

L = Leadership

Please complete the form as honestly as possible. Please answer all 40 questions. The last page also contains a summary section which should be completed by the Diagnostic Moderator.

Your Name		Your Work Area	

C = COMMUNICATION

Question	Your Score (1–7)
We use a range of communication methods (boards/briefings etc)	
I feel that I understand what is happening across the organisation	
I feel there are opportunities for me to express my views	
Communication briefings are friendly, regular and useful	
There are opportunities to discuss difficult issues in private	
Total score for Communication (min 5 — max 35):	

R = RESOURCES

Question	Your Score (1–7)
Sufficient staff have been allocated to support previous improvement projects	
Sufficient time has been allowed for programmes to succeed	
Teams focused on different aspects of improvement work well together	
I feel that improvement teams have had the resources they need	
The improvement teams have been given the capability to succeed	

I = INVOLVEMENT	
Question	**Your Score (1–7)**
When we have formed teams we have always had all the people we need	
Our projects have included relevant people from outside of our organisation	
We have actively looked for feedback from people affected by the project	
We provide opportunities for people not directly involved to express opinions	
Everyone involved feels they have an equal voice	
Total score for Involvement (min 5 — max 35):	

T = TRAINING	
Question	**Your Score (1–7)**
The amount of training we have had has been appropriate	
The quality of the training has been appropriate	
The topics covered by the training has been appropriate	
I feel I have gained the skills I need to participate in the improvement process	
I feel I understand the improvement process and my role in it	
Total score for Training (min 5 — max 35):	

I = IMPLEMENTATION	
Question	**Your Score (1–7)**
The improvement tools used are appropriate for our organisation	
The speed of implementation is appropriate for our organisation	
The way the improvement is being organised is appropriate for our organisation	
The time from undertaking training to carrying out implementation is appropriate	
The people leading the change are very knowledgeable and approachable	
Total score for Implementation (min 5 — max 35):	

C = COMPASS	
Question	**Your Score (1–7)**
We all understand where we are going with our improvement programme	
We all understand why we need to improve and believe in it	
We have a clear plan that takes us from 'here' to where we want to go	
People have had the opportunity to comment on the plan	
Our plan has believable timescales and actionable activities	
Total score for Compass (min 5 — max 35):	

A = ACHIEVEMENT

Question	Your Score (1–7)
We have made real changes to the way our services operate	
We have avoided getting stuck in 'discussions'	
The way our services are delivered have really improved	
We have celebrated our successes and shared the secrets of our success	
We feel like things are really moving for us!	
Total score for Achievement (min 5 — max 35):	

L = LEADERSHIP

Question	Your Score (1–7)
Our leadership team set the direction for improvement	
Our leadership team communicate why we are looking to make improvement	
Our leaders take an active interest in the improvement activities	
Our leaders provide useful advice and support to the programme	
Our leadership team recognise and thank successful improvement programmes	
Total score for Leadership (min 5 — max 35):	

SUMMARY SECTION – *For completion by the diagnostic coordinator*

Section	Score (max 35 per section)	Percentage (score/35x100)
Communications		
Resources		
Involvement		
Training		
Implementation		
Compass		
Achievement		
Leadership		
Totals	**Score (max of 280)**	**Percentage (score/280x100)**
Overall results		

CRITICAL Diagnostic Lite (CDL) *(Coordinator's Sheet)*

COORDINATOR'S ANALYSIS SHEET

Section	Average	Mean	Lowest Score	Highest Score	Spread
Communications					
Resources					
Involvement					
Training					
Implementation					
Compass					
Achievement					
Leadership					

Notes

Appendix 10

Who's Who – The answers from Chapter 1

Person Type	Description	Who's Who? *your guess*
Advocate	A passionate person who will sing the praises of your improvement programme	**Dr Mike Walnut**
Positive	Someone positive about the programme but who does not shout about it	**Thomas Brazil**
Neutral	Someone with an open mind and whose opinions could swing either way	**Dr Sarah Almond**
Negative	Someone who is 'anti' the programme but does not shout about it or try to influence others	**Anna Pistachio (Matron)**
Sniper	Someone who really is 'anti' and is keen to dissuade others from taking part	**Dr Gregory Pecan**
Influencer	Someone who could be any of the above categories but who also is able to influence others – sometimes called a natural leader	**Rick Hazelnut**

Printed in the United Kingdom
by Lightning Source UK Ltd.
136256UK00001B/38/P